A Writer's Guide to Guns

Also by Greg Camp:

Fiction:

No Easy Road

If You Want Peace

A Draft of Moonlight

The Willing Spirit

Non-fiction:

Each One, Teach One
(with Ranjit Singh)

Translation:

The Parliament of Fowls
(A Modern English edition of
Geoffrey Chaucer's poem)

A Writer's Guide to Guns

Greg Camp

Apollodorus Press
Fayetteville, AR
2017

ISBN: 978-1979025171

Printed in the United States

This is for informational purposes. No warranty, implied or explicit, is given, and readers are directed to use their own judgement when employing anything found herein.

Dedication:

To Sharie, who stands with me

Image Credits:

All images are used courtesy of Wikimedia Commons.

The following are from the named authors:

Page 62: http://aliengearholsters.com

Page 71: Commander Zulu

Page 89 and 90: Martin Meise

Page 94: Askild Antonsen

Page 100: Michael E Cumpston

Page 100 and 106: Hmaag

Prologue

This is not a book intended to teach anyone how to use firearms. I am not giving legal or practical advice in matters of self-defense, hunting, or competitive shooting. While it is true that you, dear reader, may learn such things by accident as you read these pages, the burden is on you to add to and test such knowledge with other sources and mentors if you want to put it into use in your own life.

The purpose herein is to provide writers with information about firearms, a subject that too often is treated in ignorance or with outright contempt by the creators of fiction—Hollywood being a prime offender. It's true that many readers will have no idea when errors get made, but that's a poor excuse for authors, especially ones who care enough about their craft to study the

         Greg Camp

intricacies of everything but guns when preparing to write.

And so, submitted for your approval, is this introduction to the vast world of firearms. It is by no means complete, as that would require a library, but it does provide a solid basis for getting started and some correctives against potential faux pas.

Keep reading, keep writing, and good luck to all my fellow writers.

Classes of Firearms

You've probably heard the expression, the pen is mightier than the sword.

This phrase was given to us by the same fellow who coined, "It was a dark and stormy night. . . ." Yes, that latter saying goes on. And on. And on. Its author was one Sir Edward George Earle Bulwer-Lytton, 1st Baron Lytton, and with a name like that, perhaps wordiness was to be expected. But too often, the mighty pen fails when describing the sword—or the firearm, as will be the point of this book.

When I first entered the Gun Nut Forest, as retired gun blogger, Kim du Toit called it—a territory both vast and varied with many climates, cultures, and crannies—I found a webpage by speculative fiction writer, William Sanders, that introduced

me to a great many subjects that people too often get wrong when it comes to guns. Alas, that site is now dark, and so, in my own version of apostolic succession, I'm going to offer a guide to gunpowder weapons for writers.

Why is this necessary? Because too many get the subject wildly wrong. Now this is not unique to firearms. There are an unfortunate number of scribblers who are laboring under the opinion that research isn't necessary. Sorry, but that's the wrong answer. If you're going to write a story about a time and a place, you need to know pages of material about such for every sentence you put in. Unless the story is science fiction or the like, I don't want to see airplanes that flap their wings to fly. Yes, that has been done, but we're talking a rare thing here, and there isn't a regular passenger service using that technique. Yes, I also know that Shakespeare and Chaucer wrote stories about the Trojan War as though the conflict happened in their own times, but unless you can write at their level, you'd better not tell me a story about Alexander the Great using stirrups, for example–unless you've got a whole lot of 'splainin' done to justify it.

All right. Where to begin? We'll start with the categories of firearms as found in common use today:

1. Rifle

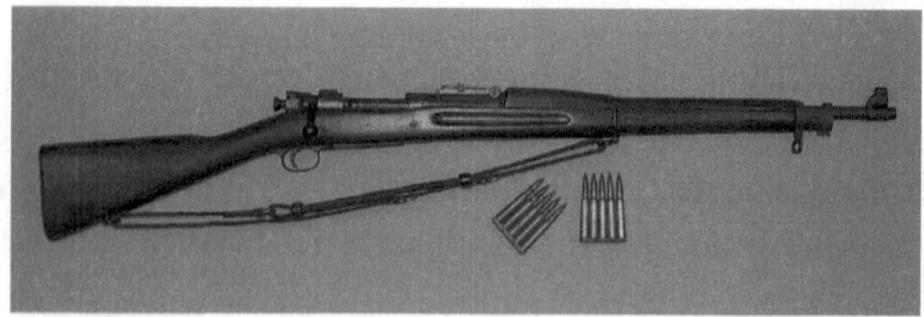

That particular beauty is a Springfield M1903, one of the long arms issued to American soldiers in the First and Second World Wars. The term is an example of synecdoche, using a part of the thing to describe the whole. Rifling is something done to the inside of the barrel whereby spiraling grooves are cut into the metal, causing the bullet to spin as it goes down, giving it gyroscopic motion, much like a spinning football, stabilizing the projectile's flight path. The word can also mean to ransack or steal, and both meanings come from a word in Middle French that meant scrape or scratch.

A rifle is a long gun. That means that it's, well, long, but it also means that you fire it with the butt of the stock (the back end) against your shoulder, and you use two hands to hold it. Can it be fired from the hip with one hand? Perhaps, but that's not any wiser than looking down the barrel to see if something's going to come out. The fact that it's long doesn't by itself affect the accuracy, but the length of barrel does give the powder used time to burn more fully, thereby increasing the velocity of the bullet. Jeff Cooper–retired Marine, firearms expert, and all-around man from another age–called the rifle the queen of personal weapons in his book, *The Art of the Rifle*. Depending on the type of cartridge used, a rifle can hit targets at over a thousand yards, and one good hit is enough to stop an animal, human or otherwise, or break machinery.

Rifles fire these:

We'll talk more in a later chapter about classes of cartridges.

2. Shotgun

This is also a long gun, though sometimes we see short versions. Old-timers also called this a scattergun, and therein lies a problem. First, have a look at one type:

This is the Winchester Model 1897, invented by John Moses Browning, a person you'll hear about repeatedly in the Gun Nut Forest. (He and a fellow from Austria named Glock are responsible for a huge swath of modern firearms.) The shotgun fires shells:

The shell contains pellets or a single slug (or other things) that are fired down a smooth tube, unlike the grooved barrel of a rifle. (There are a few rifled shotguns, but those are uncommon.) The pellets tend to spread out one inch per yard of travel, though there are variations in that. This means that the effective reach of a shotgun is well under fifty yards with pellets, though a slug (a big chunk of lead) can hit what is wanted a bit farther out. The fact that those projectiles aren't accurate past that distance doesn't mean that they aren't still dangerous.

But close in—inside a room or within conversational distance—the pellets are bunched up together. You can't vaguely point a shotgun in the general direction of your target and expect to achieve the desired results. Shotguns have to be aimed. The fact that the pellets spread out does mean that the target in range gets a bunch of holes in it per shot, instead of just one hole.

3. Handgun

As indicated by the name, a handgun is used by the hand. No shoulder involved. Typically in days gone by, only one hand was used, though decades ago, Jack Weaver and the aforementioned Jeff Cooper, et al. taught us that a two-handed grip is better for control and accuracy.

Handguns fall into two categories, revolver and self-loading:

A. Revolver

This type was invented in the first half of the nineteenth century by Samuel Colt, though there were attempts at the same thing that came before. It has a cylinder that holds cartridges

and revolves (surprise, surprise, surprise), bringing one cartridge at a time in line with the barrel to be fired.

Revolvers—a Smith & Wesson Model 10 in the picture—are fired by a hammer—in the picture, that's the spur at the rear above the grip. Cocking the gun means pulling back the hammer till it locks into place, waiting to be released by the trigger. Early revolvers had to be cocked as a separate process, but most today can be cocked and fired by squeezing the trigger in one motion. More about that later.

Though there have been some rare exceptions, most revolvers do not have external safeties. This means no thumb lever, no switch, and no catch to disengage before squeezing the trigger. We'll talk about revolvers and safeties in the future, but for now, just take it that revolvers don't have safeties. They typically carry five or six rounds, but as always, there are other possibilities.

B. Self-loading

This type is problematic in naming. They used to be called automatics. Today, they're called semiautomatics. They're also known as self-loaders. What do we mean? First, have a look at one popular example, an M1911:

and another, a Glock:

These are loaded with a box called a magazine that fits into the grip. When the trigger is squeezed, the force of the firing cartridge pushes the top part of the gun, called the slide, back, ejecting the empty cartridge case and picking up another one from the magazine to insert into the chamber, the rear end of the barrel.

Some of these have external safeties, while others do not. On the M1911, note the lever at the rear just below the hammer. When the hammer is cocked, the safety can be engaged, blocking

the gun from firing. The Glock, by contrast, only has a lever on the trigger itself. If you're going to write about automatic pistols, know exactly which kind and how it works, since there are many variations.

Those are the basic types of firearms used today. There are many subcategories and some oddball things here and there, and we've yet to get into guns of days gone by, but this is good enough to be going on with. In discussions to follow, we'll get into the details.

Cartridges

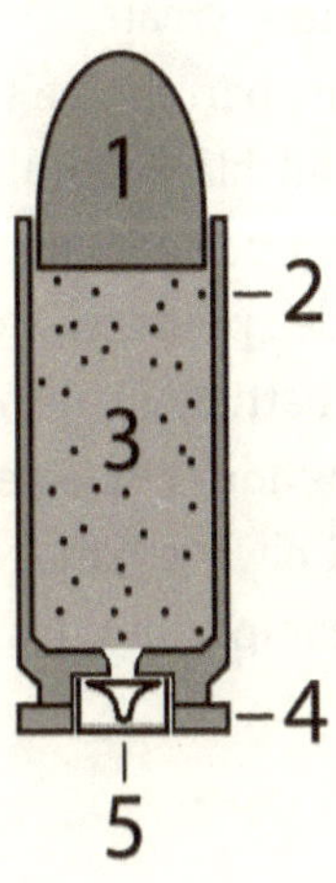

To continue the discussion of firearms from the perspective of the writing craft, we have to address the facts about ammunition. In the last chapter, I listed the common types of firearms used now. Here we'll look at what those guns shoot.

The first thing is to clarify terminology. A lot of words get tossed around with regard to what gets fed into and fired out of a gun, especially by people whose interest is banning rather than understanding. But properly speaking, we're talking about cartridges. Consider the diagram:

1. Bullet

Typically made of lead, though other materials are being used increasingly, thanks to concerns over environmental pollution, and often covered with a jacket of a copper alloy. This is what is sent down the barrel and on out to do work over down range.

2. Case

These days usually made of brass, though again, other metals can be used. Ammunition made in Russia is often steel cased, and using steel reduces cost. The case contains the other components until they're fired.

3. Powder

This is the fuel. When ignited, its burning creates rapidly expanding gases that push the bullet down the barrel. The term, gunpowder, used to mean what we today call black powder, a mixture of saltpeter, sulfur, and charcoal. Most powders now are what is called smokeless powder. Black powder produces clouds of white smoke that made seeing on the battlefield difficult, along with the odor possessed by hydrogen sulfide—some people call that a "rotten egg smell," but let's avoid clichés. Smokeless powder isn't entirely without smoke, but in comparison, it's well named.

4. Rim

Between the rim and the main body of the case is a groove. Most firearms have a claw, called an extractor, that fits into that groove to eject the case when the mechanism of the gun is opened. If the rim has the same diameter as the rest of the case, it's called rimless. (Did you expect these terms to make sense?) If it sticks out slightly, it's semi-rimmed, and a wide and obvious rim is called rimmed. (So you did expect it to make sense...)

5. Primer

This is what ignites the powder. It gets struck by the hammer or by a spring-loaded internal pin. Primers contain a shock-sensitive explosive that goes off with a hot enough flash to set the stable powder alight. This part is also called a cap. That goes back to the middle years of the nineteenth century when primers were a separate component. The phrase, bust a cap, comes from that period as well.

The priming method today is divided into rimfire and centerfire:

The dents shown on the cases in the picture are where the hammer or firing pin struck the case. A rimfire round has the explosive compound in a ring around the inside of the rim, while the centerfire concentrates it in a central cap. Rimfire cases aren't as strong as centerfire cases, so

the former, most often a .22, isn't as powerful as the latter.

You'll hear people refer to cases as brass, particularly in police procedural shows or books—an officer at a crime scene, say, will be looking for brass. Those are the spent cases. Another term for cartridges or for the bullets themselves is rounds, a name that comes from the days when bullets were primarily round balls.

Bullets come in a variety of forms, but they fit into the following general categories, from left to right:

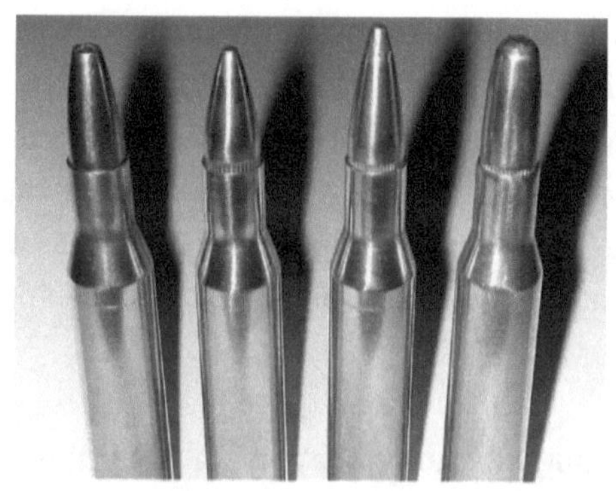

1. Hollow point

The front end of the bullet is hollow. This has two purposes. One involves the physics of motion through air. The hollow tip improves the bullet's stability, making the round stay on target. The main purpose, though, is to cause the bullet to expand inside a target, thereby doing more damage and making the round count. Hollow point rounds—especially when fired from a handgun—are more likely to stop inside the target, rather than blowing on through.

2. Full metal jacket

Remember Stanley Kubrick's film? The title comes from the fact that many militaries are required to use rounds that are made of lead that is completely covered by a jacket of copper alloy. This is due to the Hague Conventions (not Geneva!) on the laws of war. Some figured that a full metal jacket round is more humane. Such a round tends to punch through a target and head on toward whatever else is on the other side, making them bad for self-defense or hunting, but these cartridges are generally cheaper and make good practice ammunition.

3. Soft tip

These have their lead cores exposed partway. They function somewhat like hollow points in that the shape of the bullet gets distorted in the target, but that shape also allows for deeper penetration.

4. Round nose

This is an old style, found today in handgun rounds, but not so often for rifles, unless used in a tubular magazine (more on that later).

Some cartridges have what's called frangible bullets. Those are made of metal powder that's glued together. The bullets blow apart on impact, causing much less penetration. Those are used by air marshals, for what may be an obvious reason, and also in

shotgun ammunition designed to smash the hinges of doors for breaching, entering a room by force.

Sometimes, these rounds are called shells. That can be confusing, since the term is also commonly used to refer to shotgun ammunition:

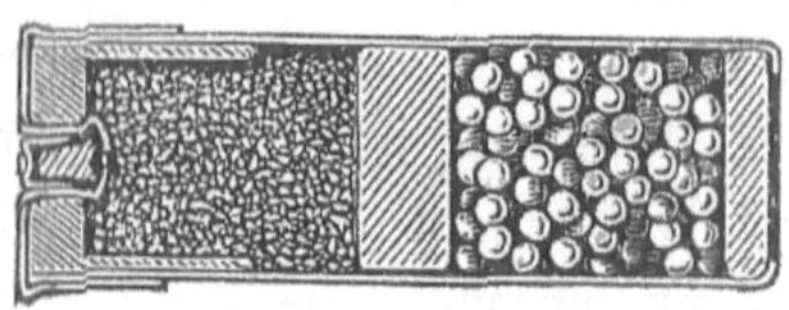

Notice that here, we have the same primer and powder and case arrangement—though the primer is a different size, and the case is typically made of plastic—but the shotgun shell adds wadding over the powder and over the shot pellets. Those pellets are used instead of a single bullet, unless we're talking slugs, which are single bullets. (Did I mention that things are complicated in the Gun Nut Forest?) As I mentioned in the last chapter, pellets tend to spread out one inch per yard of travel.

Shotgun shells are big and long and plastic, and so are easy to distinguish from rifle or handgun cartridges. That's only true today, though. If you're writing westerns, you'll need to know about metal shells.

Shotguns are classified by their bore diameters according to an old system. If you read Patrick O'Brian's Aubrey/Maturin series, you'll hear ship's guns referred to by the weight of ball that they shot. An eight pounder gun, for example, shot an iron ball weighing eight pounds. No human being could hold such a gun. Shotgun bore sizes are actually fractions of a pound. A twelve gauge, then, means a gun that could fire a solid lead ball that weighs 1/12 of a pound. The diameter is around .73 inches. A twenty gauge would shoot a ball 1/20 of a pound in weight. Thus the bigger the gauge number, the smaller the diameter. I've seen news articles describing a .12 gauge shotgun, but that's a typo, since the gun would fire an 8 1/3 pound ball.

The classification of rifle and handgun rounds is complicated, but one way to simplify things is to remember that rifle rounds are long, while handgun rounds are short:

The one on the left is for a rifle; the one on the right is for a handgun. But then there's the one in the middle. That's used in the AK-47 and other guns. It's an intermediate (in the middle, get it?) round. The longer the case, the more powder it can hold. Longer is generally more powerful.

But all three of those are the same caliber, namely .30 inches. Caliber simply means the diameter of the barrel or the bullet. (As always, there are complications, but we'll leave those aside for now.) Rifle calibers are usually a good indication of the diameter. A .308 Winchester, for example, shoots a bullet of about .308 inches. Listing rifles in order of their calibers is a

rough way to organize them by power, though you have to remember that for a given caliber, the longer the case, the more powerful the cartridge, and even within the same caliber, there can be many different lengths of cases.

With handguns, things are a mess.

Here's a list of typical cartridges in order of the diameter of their bullets:

.22
.25
.32 S&W, .32 A.C.P., 7.62 Tokarev
.380, .38 Special, .357 Magnum, 9mm Luger, .357 Sig
9mm Makarov
.40 S&W, 10mm
.44 Russian, .44 Special, .44 Magnum
.45 Colt, .45 A.C.P.

The .32s are about one third of an inch, and the group that starts with .380 are all around .355 inches. The .44s are actually .429 in diameter. This in part is the result of the fact that in the Old West days, the designation came from measuring at a different place from where we measure today. But in terms of power, things are all over the map. A .25, for example, is about the same as a .22. While a .357 Magnum bullet is the same diameter as a .38 Special (and a .357 revolver can fire .38 Specials), the case of the former is longer and holds more powder. Speaking of news articles, sometimes I see a .9mm referred to. The decimal point there is wrong, since in English terms, that's 0.03543 inches, the diameter of a middling hypodermic needle.

The short version of this long talk is that we'll discuss power later on. For now, understand that handgun caliber doesn't tell you everything you need to know about how much punch is coming out the business end.

Gun people sometimes talk about feeding their guns. This long discussion shows what we mean. As you can see, guns have specific diets. This isn't too complicated, so long as you remember that you need to know what the particular gun you're writing about happens to use. When cats drink milk, they get looseness of the bowels. The same occurs to our stories when we don't do research. But with this guide, at least you now know where to get started.

Cartridge Power

In the previous chapter, I touched briefly on the subject of power. This time, that's the focus. Power comes from three factors: shape, velocity, and mass. We'll take those one at a time.

1. Shape

The shape of the bullet makes a difference in what it does inside the target. Hollow point rounds, when moving at a high enough speed, open up, thereby tearing a bigger hole, but penetrating less distance. Spitzer rounds—bullets with spire points—tend to go straight through whatever they hit, though the lighter weight ones can tumble, such as what can happen with the 5.56 NATO or .223 round (the metric and English units are actually for different cartridges of the same diameter that are almost identical, but have minor differences that aren't important with regard to the power) fired by the AR-15. Long bullets penetrate more than short bullets (get your mind out of the gutter) in the way that a dump truck will hurt you, but a freight train will keep on hurting you. The infamous 6.5 Carcano round, for example, has a narrow diameter, .25 inches, but a long body.

What the bullet does in the target is called terminal ballistics. The shape of the bullet also affects how it moves through the air. This is known as external ballistics. Bullets with a round nose tend to be less stable than spitzer bullets, and pointy bullets with a hollow tip are more stable still. The bullet is lighter on the front end, shifting the center of mass back, stabilizing it. (That's how the U.S. military gets around the Hague Convention's ban on expanding ammunition—it's for the trajectory, you see, not for the end effect.)

2. Velocity

This may seem simple, but it's more than just how much speeding a speeding bullet does. On that subject, the velocity is typically given in feet per second or meters per second, if you're on the metric system. That's how many units of distance the bullet will travel in one second.

The faster the bullet goes, the sooner it reaches out and touches something, but there's more, as you might expect. In high school physics, there's often a thought experiment about a hunter sitting in a tree who spots a monkey at his height in another tree. Should the hunter aim above, below, or right at the monkey, presuming the monkey lets go of the tree and drops

toward the ground when the shot is fired? The answer is to aim right at the animal, since gravity affects the monkey and the bullet the same way when the bullet is fired horizontally. This is bullet drop, and you can consult Galileo and Newton for more on the subject. It's the reason that the sights on a gun are actually not precisely parallel to the barrel. They create a slight rise in the bullet's trajectory, and more on that in the chapter on accuracy. If they didn't, the round would drop into the earth long before one second was up. (Objects with no upward force acting on them fall thirty-two feet in the first second in Earth's gravity.) The faster a bullet starts out, the more momentum it has, thus helping it overcome air resistance, and the longer it goes before coming to the ground.

But there's a curious effect that bullets going more than two thousand feet per second tend to have. When they hit soft tissue, they generate a shock wave, called hydrostatic shock, that causes massive damage even in areas that the bullet did not touch. Handgun rounds typically don't move rapidly enough to do this, while rifle rounds generally are above that threshold for a good deal of their flight. A thirty caliber handgun round, such as the .32 S&W Long, will make a hole .312 inches in diameter, while a .30-'06 round (thirty caliber, adopted in 1906) will create a big cavity inside a body after punching the same .312 inch hole, even if the two bullets have the same weight.

Another effect of velocity is to determine whether hollow point rounds will open up. Today's bullets are designed to open at lower velocities, but a general truism is that faster makes for better expansion. The speed also affects penetration. A compact car that's roaring down the highway will hit you harder than a train that's barely moving, even though the train will be more insistent.

Velocity is determined by how much powder is pushing how much mass. If the weight remains the same, more powder means more speed. Heavier bullets go slower than lighter bullets with the same amount of powder. Well, sort of. Powder charges do funny things. One fact from internal ballistics—what happens inside the firearm—is that a longer barrel gives more time for the powder to burn behind the bullet, rather than out in open air. Of course, there comes a point at which all the powder is burned, but within limits, the longer the barrel, the faster the bullet will go. We carry short-barreled firearms for convenience, not because they are more effective.

3. Mass

Bullet mass is measured in grains, of which there are seven thousand in a pound. Look at the picture of rifle cartridges in the last chapter again. Those are .270 caliber rounds. The first on the left is 100 grains, the next 115, the one after that 130, and the last is 150. The heavier a bullet is, the more it adds to the constant part, M, of the $F = MV$ equation and thus the higher F, or force, will be for more of the trajectory. Heavy bullets punch through the wind better, and they tend to be more stable. That stability can be good, if the bullet has to penetrate tough material, but it also doesn't tumble in soft tissue, meaning the round just goes on through, instead of staying inside to be useful. To use the train metaphor again, the first bullet is the engine, while each successive bullet adds more cars behind.

What does this all add up to?

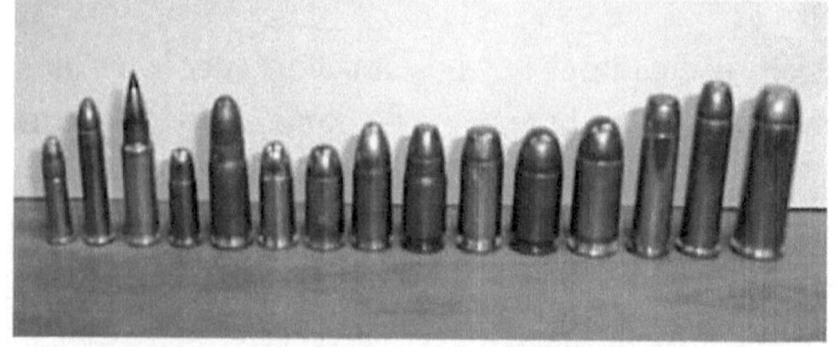

Note the second and third cartridges from the right. The third is a .38 Special, while the second is a .357 magnum. They both have bullets of the same diameter—the .38 number comes from an older style of bullet—and those bullets are often the same weight, but the .38 Special comes with less powder. Thus the .357 Magnum is faster. The family of .380 ACP, 9mm Luger, and .357 Sig—the last one being in the center of the picture—all are .355 in diameter, but that list is in order from least to greatest in power, thanks to how much fuel is behind the ball. The .357 Sig round in fact has a bottleneck case—the lower part of the case is broader than the neck—allowing for a greater charge.

This matters to you as a writer because knowing what a bullet will do down range makes for more realistic fiction. Remember the episode of *Breaking Bad* when—spoiler alert—Jessie shoots Gale? The kid uses a .380 ACP, and the bullet goes through Gale's head and into a metal pot on the stove at the other side of the room. Yeah, maybe, but a 9mm Luger round would have been more believable. Certainly, one staple of Hollywood that seems to be dying off now is the bullet that knocks its victim clean out of Dodge. A guy who is off balance to begin with may topple over when shot, but if the round can send a person flying, the force of the cartridge firing would send the shooter just as far in the other direction. Recoil can be stout, but in the real world, it's not that bad.

The key point of this chapter is to provide a sense of how bullets act. They are physical objects only, not rings of power or any other magical thing, and writers who include gun play in their stories ought to have some sense of what's possible and what's cartoonish.

Triggers

In the Gun Nut Forest, you'll hear lots of terms for the characteristics of the trigger. We'll start with what it does. There are two kinds of trigger actions, single:

and double:

Notice that the double-action trigger is in the middle of the trigger guard, while the single-action trigger is near the back? There's a reason for this. The double-action variety has more work to do, often.

Double action used to be the way of saying that you could fire the gun in two ways—either by cocking the hammer yourself first and dropping it with a short squeeze of the trigger or simply by pulling the trigger back and letting it cock the hammer for you and then drop it. Single-action triggers only drop the hammer. You have no choice but to cock those on your own.

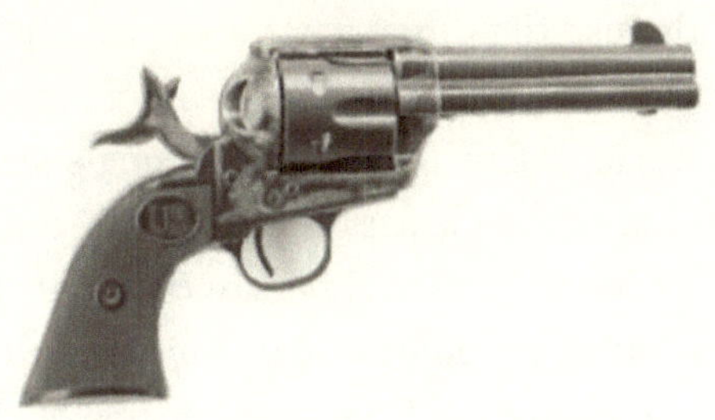

or to let the slide cock the hammer for you during the firing stroke.

These days, double action is mainly used to describe the firing mode whereby the trigger does all the work—to say that the trigger has twice the number of jobs. Thus we hear about double-action-only guns. Properly speaking, that's a single action, since there's only one way to fire the beast, but using the trigger to cock and fire is what people now generally mean by double action.

Single-action triggers are easier to work than double action, since there's less for the trigger to do. This makes the pull weight lighter. But double action isn't too hard to learn. It just takes practice and a good hold on the gun. When we talk about safeties, we'll discuss the difference between these two actions again. All rifles and shotguns that I'm aware of are single action. Handguns come in many flavors, from single-action-only to double/single—the first shot uses the trigger to cock the action and then fire, while subsequent shots are cocked by the working of the slide—to double-action-only to mix-and-match.

But what do I mean by pull weight? Imagine holding the gun

pointing directly up and then picture a string tied to the trigger. (Don't look into the barrel, and don't do this without checking to demonstrate that the gun is unloaded!) The pull weight is however much weight would have to be on that string to pull the trigger all the way back to break—in other words, the moment when the mechanism inside releases the hammer or firing pin.

Several terms show up at this point relating to what the trigger is doing. Travel is how far it has to go from start to break. Double-action mode gives you a long row to hoe and can show stacking, the build-up of weight as things compress inside the gun. The single-action distance is much shorter. Overtravel is when the trigger keeps going past the let off (the break), and creep or grit is the friction while the trigger is in motion. Then there's reset, the distance that the trigger has to go forward before it's ready to work again.

Creep and overtravel are things that a trigger wouldn't have in an ideal world. In our world, they are things that a gunsmith sometimes can correct and that expensive handguns shouldn't have much of. Travel is a mixed blessing. A long trigger pull can be a safety measure, particularly if the gun has nothing else keeping it from firing, since long gives you more time to realize that the bang switch is caught on something–such as the finger of an owner who's not too bright–than short does.

We started out with two categories. Now we must go to three:

1. Single-stage triggers

This means that squeezing the trigger either feels the same all the way back or shows a continuous increase in pressure to

break. Shotguns have this kind of trigger, as do many rifles. Handguns often do as well, especially in double-action mode. If the trigger is particularly light in pull weight, it's jokingly called a hair trigger, meaning that a hair falling on it is enough to set it off. This is good for accuracy, since having to work at the trigger can shift the direction of the muzzle, but it can unsettle the nerves if you're walking around with the thing ready to go at the slightest provocation.

2. Two-stage triggers

These have two steps on the way to break. The squeeze is light until a point when the required pressure changes. That first part is the take-up. This is often found in military rifles, since soldiers have to run about on battlefields, and the brass figure that a gun with too light a trigger in one stage is an invitation to friendly fire. Of course, if you keep your finger off the trigger until you're ready for business, things will go better for you.

Two stages, though, isn't bad on a rifle. A long gun is meant to be held with two hands against your shoulder, and a rifle is typically at least twice as heavy as a handgun. Take-up in a pistol, especially in those with plastic bodies, can throw off your aim.

3. Set triggers

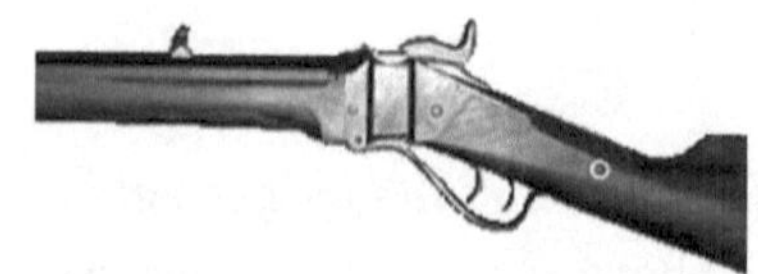

In the closeup view of that fine old Sharps buffalo gun, see the two triggers. Those aren't for two barrels, as one might find on a shotgun. The front trigger will fire the gun whenever the action is cocked, but pulling the rear trigger sets everything up to go, leaving the front ready for the slightest pressure. That's a double-set trigger. Another arrangement is to have one trigger that can be pressed forward to set for light weight, but will go off regardless when pulled to the rear. The purpose is to have the firearm ready to shoot with a heavy enough trigger ordinarily so as not to go bang at every bump, while giving the option of setting a much lighter weight for precision shots at long range.

Yes, there's a lot of fuss and bother here. Working the trigger well is one of the fundamental aspects of good shooting. This is the reason that shootists who care about hitting what they want spend a lot of time dry-firing (pulling the trigger on a gun that they've checked repeatedly to know that it's empty) while lining up the sights on a target. Actually, we often talk about pulling the trigger, but that's not the best way to describe it. I've used squeeze here and elsewhere, and that's better. The Platonic ideal is one smooth rearward contraction while nothing else moves. That takes practice.

For writers, this long discussion gives you details for building your characters. Is your person nervous or stone cold? Is your person a gun nut or someone who grabbed a gun in a moment of desperation? And on and on. The way you describe your characters' actions around firearms tells us a lot about their personalities.

Now you know. Sadly, the G.I. Joe cartoon wasn't right here, since knowing isn't even the beginning of the book. And plenty of knowing is left to come.

Revolvers

In the discussion of classes of firearms, I told you that handguns fall into two subcategories: self-loaders and revolvers. The self-loaders will be discussed in the next chapter on action types. This is on the latter of those two:

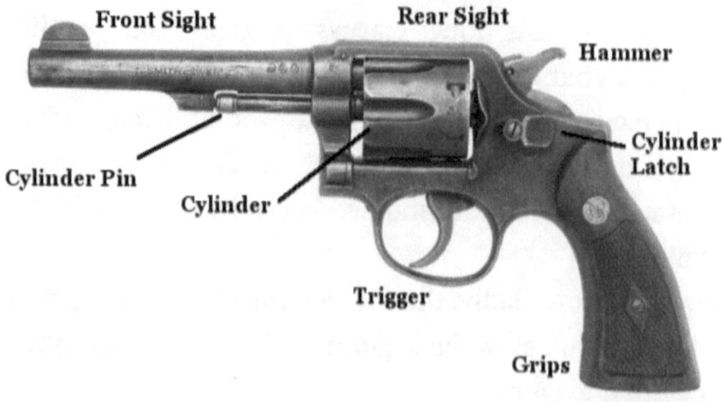

This is typical of the breed, a six-shot, double-action Smith & Wesson Model 10. Six shot means that the cylinder has six chambers, the typical number for revolvers. Double action, we discussed already. Revolvers generally are chambered in a variety of calibers, including .45 Colt, .45 ACP, .38 Special, and .357 Magnum.

Attempts at making this type of firearm go back to the early days of firearms, such as this model from the 1500s:

Over the next centuries, other attempts were made, but the first practical and working model was invented by Samuel Colt, reportedly after watching a ship's wheel:

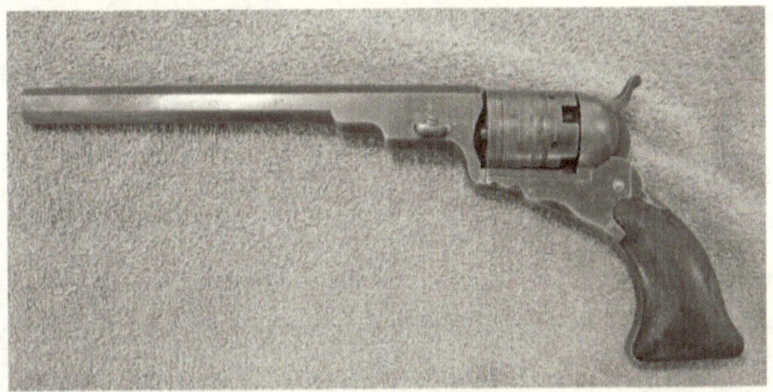

That's the Paterson model, named for the city in New Jersey where Colt's plant was located in the 1830s. (Yes, New Jersey used to understand the Second Amendment.) It had a trigger that folded up until the hammer was cocked, and the mechanism

for turning the cylinder was complicated, but it allowed its owner to have five shots available, instead of just one, allowing the Texas Rangers to surprise the Comanches in the Battle of Bandera Pass.

A stronger and simpler firearm came after Texas Ranger Captain Walker discussed the matter with Colt:

Note the loading lever beneath the barrel. The Patersons didn't have those at first, though some came with the addition later on. These are front-loading firearms, requiring powder to be poured into the open chamber and then a bullet to be rammed in by the lever. The rear of the chamber is covered by a nipple onto which a primer cap is placed. The phrase, bust a cap, comes from this period, not from modern gangsters.

And yes, those things were called nipples, though polite people used the term, cone. They are removed for cleaning by a nipple wrench and cleared of powder fouling by a nipple prick.

Have we returned from thoughts of BSDM yet?

Another famous firearms company, Smith & Wesson, came up with a series of revolvers that used self-contained cartridges instead of loose powder and ball:

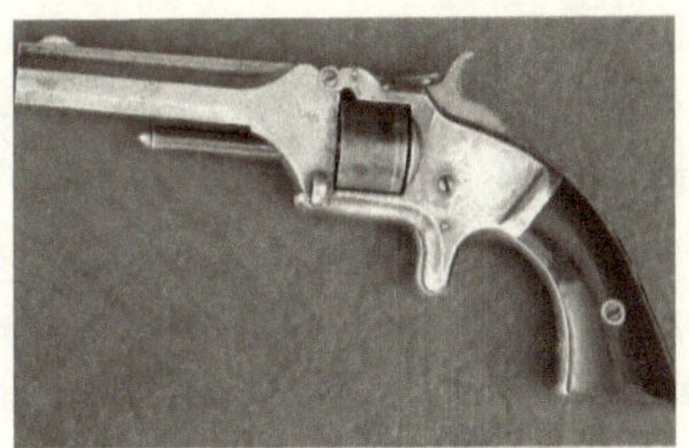

The definitive cartridge revolver of the Old West, though, was the Colt Single Action Army:

There is a fact about all of these that many have forgotten in our modern age of lawsuits and histrionics. The firing pin was on the hammer, and nothing kept it from being in contact with a primer when the hammer rested on a live chamber. This meant that under normal circumstances, the hammer was carried down on an empty chamber, making those six-guns actually five shots in practical terms. I've read somewhere that at least some pistoleroes rolled up dollar bills in the top chamber in case they needed to pay for their own funerals.

Modern revolvers typically have some mechanism to keep the firing pin off the primer, often by a blocking device to hold the hammer off until the trigger is squeezed. An old timer in your

stories might still load only five in a six-gun, but that's casting your character as out of step with the modern world (and good on you for doing so). Best practice today is to load a modern revolver all the way and go in health.

Another aspect that comes up when revolvers appear in a story is whether or not they have safeties. I've already mentioned the firing pin block. But hardly any revolver has a safety lever that has to be disengaged. Gun nuts refer to these guns as the original point-and-click interface. It's ready to go, and nothing gets in its way.

There have been some safeties on revolvers, though. One model, the Smith & Wesson Lemon Squeezer (that's a nickname, in case you're wondering), used a grip safety:

This is similar to the M1911, but it's disengaged when the shooter takes hold of the gun, so there's no thought involved.

But as always in the Gun Nut Forest, there's something out there that throws a spanner in the works. Behold, the Webley-Fosbery:

It's a semiautomatic revolver. Yup, that means that when one round fires, the barrel-cylinder-hammer arrangement slides backward under recoil, cocking the hammer and rotating the cylinder by means of a stud that works through the zig-zag cuts. Since this was a single-action gun, it had to be carried cocked to be ready for use, thus the lever at the top of the grip—a gen-u-ine thumb safety. Your characters aren't likely to have one of these, but they have shown up in *The Maltese Falcon*, one of the greats of detective fiction, whether novel or movie, and in *Zardoz*, a thoroughly dreadful film starring Sean Connery in a diaper when he decided that he was, in fact, not James Bond.

I've already told you how the front-loaders got fed. The Single Action Army and some others of the period had a loading gate to the right rear of the cylinder that allowed one round to be

inserted at a time, once the hammer had been pulled back to half cock. To go off half-cocked, by the way, means to fire when you're not supposed to. This was a slow process, one of the reasons that figures of the Old West often

carried more than one handgun. They weren't usually firing both at once. The point was to have a second gun available when the first one went dry. (This practice today is called a New York reload, but don't use that term in a western.)

Some revolvers, such as the Webleys, whether the Fosbery model or the standard versions, broke open at the top and kicked out all the shells in the same manner as a top-break shotgun.

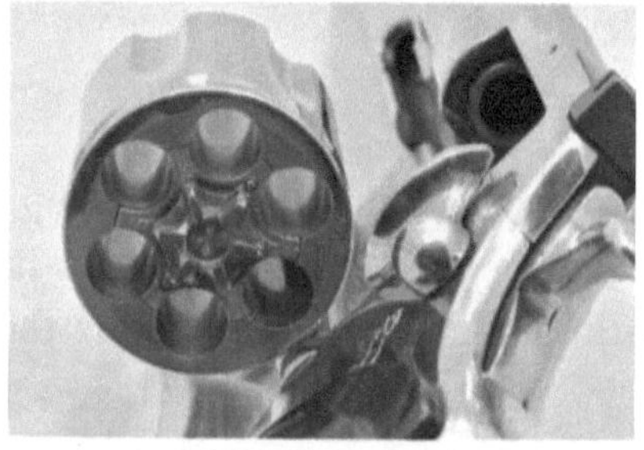

But modern revolvers mostly have a cylinder that swings out when released by the latch. The cylinder can be loaded with a speedloader or by inserting one round at a time.

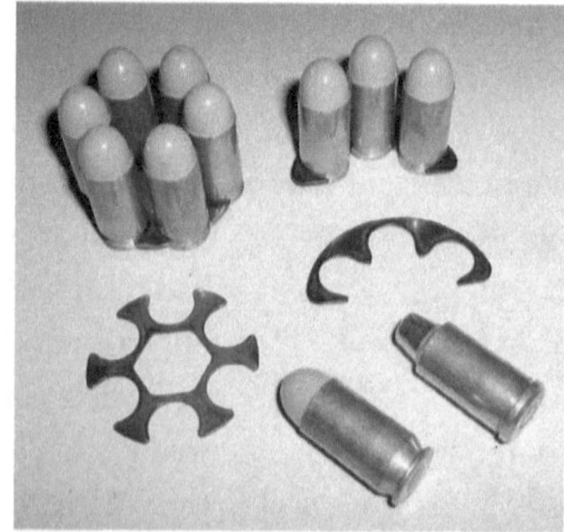

The cartridges used in revolvers typically have to be rimmed, though moon clips allow rimless cartridges to be used.

So here you've had a quick tour of Wheelgun Hollar in the Gun Nut Forest. Revolvers are seen by some as old-fashioned these days, but since they don't require the force of the firing cartridge to operate (minus the Webley-Fosbery), they aren't sensitive to the power of the round. A light target load and a hot magnum load will both work, so long as the shooter can cock and fire.

Many in this world carry revolvers as backup guns, but if your character packs a wheelgun as a primary sidearm, you're painting said person as someone who cares not at all about fitting into modern styles. I'll like you for doing that.

Action

Just as there are many cartridges in the Gun Nut Forest, there are also many actions. By action I mean the way the firearm operates. The first distinction to be made is between single-shot and repeaters.

1. Single shot

This means that the firearm has to be reloaded by the shooter after each shot. From the first guns in the Middle Ages to the nineteenth century, this is how just about everything worked. But such weapons are still with us, among hobbyists and some hunters.

A. Muzzleloaders

These are also called front stuffers, and that tells you exactly what loading many of them is like. The procedure for that, whether we're talking the handguns shown above all the way to the biggest cannon of the period, was to send powder down the barrel through the muzzle—either by pouring it or shoving a packet in—ram home a round, again down the muzzle and often with a cloth wad between it and the powder, and add priming powder to the charge hole at the back of the barrel. The example in the picture is a flintlock, which means that when the trigger is squeezed, the piece of flint in the hammer snaps down to strike a steel plate. The resulting sparks ignite the priming powder, and that sets off the main charge, launching the bullet. Matchlock guns had a burning cord that was brought into contact with the primer, while wheellock guns used a spring-loaded mechanism like a Zippo lighter—and were about as reliable. Once the weapon had fired, the whole loading business had to be done again, often with the addition of running a sponge or patch through the barrel to make sure that no burning embers remained.

If you've seen someone in a movie blow across the muzzle of a gun, this is why. Black powder becomes sticky when it burns

and can leave behind partially consumed residue that is still glowing. Blowing across the muzzle has the same effect as wind moving across a chimney—it accelerates the combustion. But doing so with a gun using modern powders is an act of bravado with no other utility.

B. Breechloaders

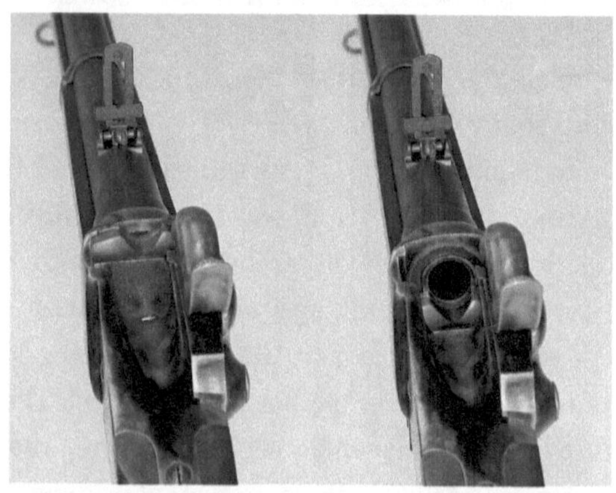

The image above is a falling-block action. That's one variety of several different means of locking the block in place for a shot, then moving it out of the way for extraction—rolling, falling, and tilting block are the common ones. In cartridge versions of the Sharps rifle—think *Quigley Down Under*—the trigger guard was also a lever that opened the action to extract the spent shell and allow a new one to be loaded. Falling-block actions are strong, since the limitation on the size of the block and the receiver that it locks into are only how much a person is able to hold, and since no parts other than the hammer or striker have to move during firing, these guns have an extra measure of mechanical accuracy. (We'll talk about accuracy in more detail later.)

Another type of single-shot—or double-shot, one per barrel—breechloader is the break action. These are often seen in shotguns, particularly older models. It's also seen in some revolvers, as we discussed before. This kind is only as strong as the latching mechanism, limiting guns using it to lower pressure cartridges.

Other actions can be single-shot, including bolt action, which we'll deal with in a moment, but most of those are obsolete today.

2. Manual repeaters

Logically enough, this term refers to firearms that can have one round in the chamber and more in a magazine or cylinder. They are cycled by the shooter.

A. Revolver

We've already discussed this type. Multiple cartridges are held in the cylinder that rotates around a pin, bringing each

round successively in line with the chamber.

B. Lever action

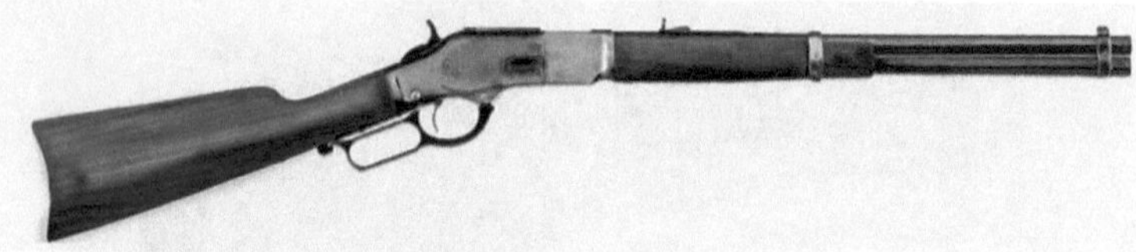

Think of every John Wayne western you've seen. Or every western, period. Sheriff Longmire carries this type of rifle in his truck. A lever gun will be the long gun that a lot of the characters in that genre carry. The one in the picture is the Winchester Model 1873, the gun that won the West, or so the movies tell us. It certainly did a lot of work in the period. If you've seen those films or if you remember the television program, *The Rifleman*, you know how this gun operates. The loop of metal attached to the trigger guard gets cranked downward to eject the shell in the chamber—straight up into the air, typically, which is why putting scopes on many lever guns is a challenge—and cycle another one in. The bolt here often is of the same type as the falling or rotating block described above.

Notice the tube under the barrel. That's not another barrel. It's the tubular magazine. (If your mind jumped immediately to "Tubular Bells" and Linda Blair spitting out pea soup, you've one strange character—and I love you for it.) Remember the bullet types?

Pointed bullets, called spitzer rounds (a round point, I know), aren't good in tubular magazines. That point can strike the primer of the next cartridge in line on recoil, setting off the whole lot of them in order. There are some lever guns that use a rotary magazine or other mechanisms, but those aren't common.

C. Pump action

This is commonly found in shotguns and also in some rifles, particularly .22 rimfire guns. The ribbed, brown slider beneath the barrel in the picture is pulled back and then forward, doing the work of ejecting one shell and chambering another. Again, if you watch movies or television, you've probably seen someone work a pump gun, accompanied by the clack-clack sound of the action. It's an impressive display, if you're impressed by displays. If the slider isn't brought all the way back and all the way forward, the cycle can hang up. That's called short-shucking.

D. Bolt action

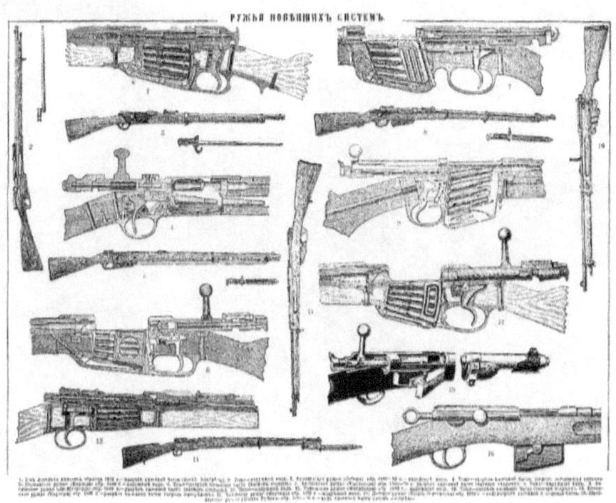

Here, the bolt, the part that has the firing pin and holds the cartridge on the bolt face, gets cycled in typically one of two ways. The usual type involves lifting the bolt handle up, pulling the bolt back to eject a shell, then pushed forward to take a round out of the magazine and into the chamber, after which the handle is pressed down again. Rifles patterned on the German Mauser design cock the action at the beginning of that process, while the Lee-Enfields of the British cock on closing. Straight-pull bolt actions are just what you'd imagine—pull back, push forward. The bolts on both types have lugs that get inserted into grooves in the receiver—the metal body of the back part of the firearm—to hold the action in place during firing. Because the bolt doesn't have to move while the round is going down the barrel, that lockup can be strong, allowing bolt actions to fire some freakish Magnum cartridges, such as the .577 Tyrannosaur, compared to a .308 Winchester round:

3. Automatic repeaters

Before we get into the details, I have to clarify that by automatic, in this context, I don't necessarily mean a "machine gun." As we discussed in the first chapter, the names get confused. Automatic, semiautomatic, and self-loader mean the same thing in terms of how the action is cycled. What gets called fully automatic or full-auto these days is a gun that will fire as long as there are rounds in the magazine and the trigger is squeezed, but that's a different matter.

Automatic repeaters use the energy of the firing cartridge to work the mechanism, either employing the direct force of recoil or the expanding gas from the burning powder. Some part of the gun—the slide, the bolt, or some other part—goes through a reciprocating motion, back and forward again.

A. Blowback

Friction holds the fired shell in the chamber long enough for the bullet to go down the barrel, and the force of the expanding gas works like rocket fuel to push that shell backward and the bolt along with it. The spent shell is then ejected, and a new one picked up when the spring forces the bolt forward again.

Recognize this gun:

Yup, that's the gun that this fellow used when he was watching birds.

No, wait, um, that guy's the ornithologist. The Walther PPK is, of course, the gun used by James Bond, the secret agent that was named after someone whose book on birds Ian Fleming had read. He's part of the clandestine services, except that everyone knows his name, his drink, and the fact that his gun shoots a pissant little round. Most blowback actions don't lock the slide and bolt together during firing, so they can't stand a lot of force. From zero to .380 (look at that snail accelerate!), the rounds are weak enough to allow this type of action to work.

There are some mechanisms that delay the blowback, such as rollers that lock the action for the beginning of the firing process, allowing for more powerful cartridges. Another option is to make the slide or bolt heavier to delay the cycling. The Tommy gun of gangster fame used that approach, though the .45 ACP that it used isn't a high pressure round.

B. Recoil operated

Another way of describing this is to call it a locked-breech action. The M1911 is an example of this type. When the slide is forward, the barrel is locked to it by lugs. Upon firing, the recoil force acting on the shell presses the slide backward. The barrel travels a bit with the slide, then is disengaged by a link or ramp or rotating lug that unlocks the barrel and slide, pulling the barrel down or turning it. The slide continues on back, ejecting the shell and stripping off a new one from the magazine when the spring pulls the slide forward again.

C. Gas operated

This category takes us into one of the hottest controversies in the Gun Nut Forest: Piston or direct impingement.

i. Piston

See the tube on top? There's a tiny hole in the barrel that allows gas to enter that tube and press on a piston that will drive the bolt backward. The AK-47, as shown, the M1 Garand, the SKS, and many other gas operated firearms use this method. The Desert Eagle pistol also uses a variation on this method.

It works, but it has several moving parts.

ii. Direct impingement

In this gun, the M-16, there's just a tube. The gas itself forces the bolt to cycle. That means one fewer moving part, which means less to throw off the aim, but if that gas is dirty—and it was in the early days of the M-16 when the choice of gunpowder was a poor one—it reminds us of the phrase, don't shit where you eat. Either the gas tube would gum up or the powder residue would gum up the bolt's channel, or this, or that, or the other. I try to remain neutral in these articles (yeah, right), but I'll point out that while I've seen piston guns firing away at the range, I've also seen many direct impingement guns being disassembled so the owner can find where the thing is stuck. That being said, when the thing is kept clean, it tends to run.

iii. Gas-delayed blowback

Think back to that wondrous Christmas movie, *Die Hard*. Remember Hans Grüber's handgun, the H&K P7:

It bleeds off some of the firing gas to press on a spring-loaded piston that holds the slide in place until the bullet leaves the barrel. (Note also the squeeze-cocking device on the grip. That has to be held compressed to keep the weapon ready to fire.)

As always, there are lots of variations on what I've described here, and there are a plenty of other designs. These are the most common actions. The astonishing thing is that these work at all. The weakest cartridges fire at more than ten thousand pounds per square inch. The power only goes up from there. But this is what happens inside the gun, and when you make choices for your characters, remember that what firearm you select says things about the person you're creating.

Fire at will, and now you know what's going on inside when you do it.

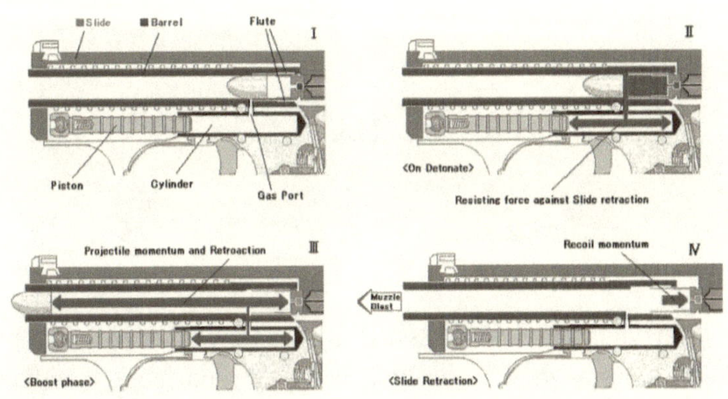

Carry

Carrying a gun isn't easy. Hollywood makes it look like no great burden to run around with an enormous handgun concealed under a form-fitting suit or dress that can be whipped out without a hitch at the slightest provocation. But a handgun is an irregularly shaped combination of metal, wood, or polymers that weighs typically a pound or more. The overall length is at least half a foot for most models, and it can go on up to well over a foot in the largest revolvers. The grip is attached at an angle from the barrel or slide, meaning that successfully concealing one part can result in the other part sticking out for all to see.

On that specific point, there are many who should know better who talk about how a short barrel makes concealment easier, when in fact it's the grips that create the biggest challenge. The barrel or slide lines up with the body in most carry methods, and the length, within reason, doesn't matter so much. The width—thickness of the slide or the cylinder in particular—makes a difference, and the handle that makes holding on to the gun easier has to be taken into account, and solving that often works at cross purposes to hiding the barrel.

Let's then consider the ways that people generally carry handguns, looking at the advantages and disadvantages of each:

1.   Pocket

Clothing years ago was better adapted to this. Pockets were deeper, and getting clothes tailored to individual requirements was more common. But even now, there are some handguns that can be carried in a pocket. Smart people will carry nothing else in that pocket for reasons that I hope are obvious.

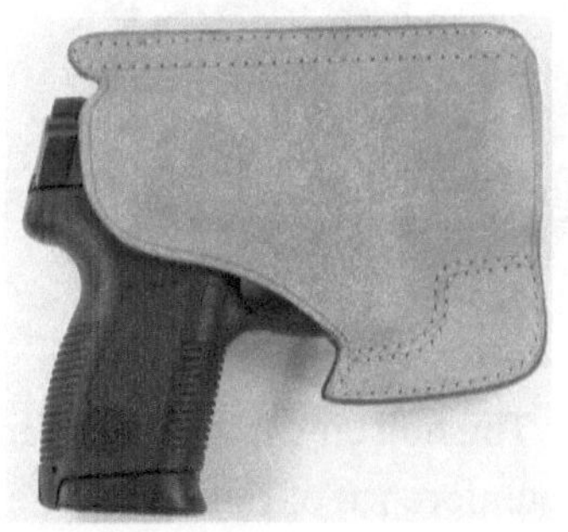

One set of problems arises from the shape of the gun and the type of cloth used. The sights on handguns often have rough edges, and after not too many times of that kind of carry, there will be holes in the pocket lining. Some guns come with rounded surfaces

Another problem is snagging while drawing the handgun. Revolvers with exposed hammers risk this, as do guns with high sights. A solution to this and the preceding problem is a pocket holster. Another answer is to shroud the hammer within the

body of the revolver.

Pocket carry allows the person to have a hand on the gun discreetly, but it does limit the options to small models. And if your dominant hand is injured, you won't have easy access to the gun.

2.   Inside the Waistband

This puts the handgun in between you and your pants. People who carry this way often have to buy a size bigger to accommodate the extra volume, though pistols like the M1911 or the Browning Hi Power are slender enough to make this easier.

The holster can be placed in a variety of positions around the circumference of the body. The tacticool folks on YouTube these days like appendix carry, which has the pistol's muzzle pointing in the vicinity of the femoral artery and the genitalia of male carriers. If your character is a lady's man, he may wish to reconsider that choice. Another bad position is called small-of-the-back carry. That puts the handgun next to the person's spine, and while smaller guns disappear in this position, the presence of a hard object there is ill-advised for anyone who might fall over backwards.

More typically, holsters for this type of carry are place between two and four o'clock for right-handed carriers or eight to ten o'clock for lefties. This puts the gun in an easy place to line up with the rest of the body, and it's in the natural position to reach for it when drawing. Access to the non-dominant hand isn't there, unless the arrangement is in a cross-draw position, in which the gun is on the opposite side of the body from the dominant hand, but oriented for that hand to grasp it.

A variation of this is the bellyband holster. Travelers in crime-ridden tourist areas have been carrying money and passports this way for a while, and some who carry firearms realized that hiding a small gun that way makes sense. Since it's done under a covering shirt, that garment has to be moved out of the way before the gun can be drawn.

3.   Outside the Waistband

This is a lot like the previous method, only—and isn't it clear from the name—that the holster is attached to the belt outside the pants. It's the way just about everyone has seen handguns be carried—uniformed cops do it. To conceal the gun this way requires an outer garment that extends beneath the holster and muzzle, and while inside-the-waistband carry tends to keep the grip pressed inward, outside lets it lean away. Gun fighters of the Old West are often pictured as carrying this way, though don't forget that many of them also had smaller revolvers hidden on their persons.

4.   Shoulder

This is called a shoulder holster because the straps run over the shoulders, though typically the handgun will be slung along the person's side. It's the method that Inspector Harry Callahan uses to carry his .44 Magnum revolver in Dirty Harry, and he's only one example of many characters to do so.

Carry this way typically requires a coat or similar garment to conceal the gun, if that's important to the character. A shoulder rig takes effort to keep the gun from poking outward, and if the coat flaps open in a breeze or during movement, the secret is exposed to anyone watching. But then, guns in or outside the waistband are shown by a rising shirt, and pocket carry gives itself away if the gun is too big or the pocket too small.

5.   Ankle

Ankle holsters are like leggings, predictably around the ankle region, though often covering more of the lower leg than just that. Much like pocket carry, this method is only good for small guns, no matter what Hollywood may have shown you. And it requires the pant leg to be wide enough to be practical and long enough to work, especially if the character sits, making the pants ride up.

The problem with ankle carry is clear if you stand and try to untie your shoes in that position. It puts the gun as far away from one's hands as is possible with the gun still on the body. This method works for people who will be rolling on the ground a good deal with their legs bent under them. It also works for people who spend a lot of time driving. And for those who like to carry several guns, making the one on the ankle a last-ditch option.

Of course, characters in the Old West would from time to time slide a small gun into their boots, and if you're sitting a horse for long periods, that's not too far out of reach.

6.   Off body

Unless we're talking about a purse or similar, this really isn't carrying, but at times, it's useful to have a handgun nearby, but not obviously on one's person. General Jack Ripper keeps his M1911 hidden under some papers on his desk for a bit while talking to Group Captain Lionel Mandrake in *Dr. Strangelove or: How I Learned to Stop Worrying and Love the Bomb*. James Bond kept a Colt Single Action Army revolver in the glove box of his Aston Martin. Michael Weston hides a Sig Sauer pistol under his sink in *Burn Notice*.

The trouble here is that the handgun is out of immediate control of its owner. In the *Stargate* franchise, Colonel Jack O'Neill's son finds his Beretta M9 and kills himself accidentally with it. Other characters in the story might run across the weapon, either while searching or by chance. But keeping a gun in a desk drawer is a comfortable choice for people whose desks aren't regularly inspected and who'd rather not have to carry their pieces all the time.

7.   Women

No, this isn't a carry method. It's an acknowledgment that the things that I've described in this chapter aren't limited to one

sex, but if your character is a woman, it's best to consider her shape and how these techniques apply.

My advice here is to spend time on a website written by Kathy Jackson, *The Cornered Cat*. She's teaches the subject of carry—and in particular how it applies to women—and can speak to it more expertly than I can.

The methods described throughout this chapter are the typical ways that people carry handguns with them in their daily lives. That's when they're not expecting a fight, but know that one could be brought to them. Convicts entering prison use other methods that I'll leave to your imagination. In any case, carry isn't easy, and you should understand that when creating your characters.

Safeties

I read a lot of the writings of commentary from those who sit outside the Gun Nut Forest and scoff about the people, regions, and activities inside. Though I'm trying not to be too political in these articles, I do wish that folks would learn the subject before going on at length about it. Thus this guide to guns. In this chapter, we're discussing safeties.

First off, let's understand that the most important safety is the one located between your ears. There are a great many mechanical devices that reduce the chances of something going wrong, but fools always find a way around any proofing. Recall that the word, idiot, was ancient Greek for someone not capable of functioning in public. We'll go through Jeff Cooper's Four Rules in another chapter, but for now, understand that if you

would laugh at some guy doing it in a movie, you shouldn't do it yourself with a real gun.

With that said, let's talk about what is used to keep a gun from going bang:

Start with the trigger. I can hear you through space and time, shouting, *¿Como que huh?* But have a look:

That's a Radom P-64, a Polish knockoff of the Walther PPK. It's trigger pull weight in factory standard is twenty-seven pounds. If you recall the chapter about triggers, you remember that pull weight means whatever weight tied to a string would be required to pull the trigger if the gun is pointing upward. I write fiction, but even I have a hard time coming up with a scenario whereby the trigger on a P-64 could get pulled by accident. The typical double-action trigger is around eight to twelve pounds—not too heavy, but usually enough to keep the gun from firing unless the person holding it intends for that to happen.

Glocks and many other handguns these days have a lever on

the trigger that has to be disengaged for the trigger to be squeezed. Of course, since that lever is on the trigger itself, it doesn't count for much, but the company calls it a Safe Action Trigger ® anyway.

But safeties typically are divided into two categories, passive and active.

1. Passive

These are safeties that the shooter doesn't have to think about. They are either switched off by holding the gun or by the natural operation in the process of firing. The Glock trigger is one example. That safety will be disengaged by doing what comes naturally.

Another example is a grip safety. The pistol to the right has a safety lever on the trigger, but also notice the one along the back of the grip. Holding the gun normally released that one, but if the gun is lying on a table, the grip safety blocks the action from working. M1911s also have this, and gun nuts argue  endlessly about whether a comfortable hold on the gun fails to deactivate the safety, but for the most part, these are a gimme.

The Colt Single Action Army and the M1911 have a half-cock notch on the hammer. One purpose of this is to provide a catch point in case the hammer gets knocked accidentally.

Other passive safeties are to be found inside many guns. One technique is to lock the firing pin until the trigger is squeezed. Another, found on many revolvers, is to separate the hammer from the firing pin, either by preventing it from traveling far enough or by using a transfer bar that stays out of the way when the trigger is forward. On self-loading pistols, some models such

as the Browning Hi Power have a disconnector that prevents the gun from firing if the magazine has been removed. All of these types can add weight to the trigger pull, so they're not always popular.

2. Active

The lever on the gun by the hammer is an example of this category. Self-loading pistols have to have a round chambered by racking the slide. That also typically cocks the hammer or the firing pin or striker. On the model in the picture, a Walther PPK, thumbing down the safety lever works as a decocker, lowering the hammer without letting it strike the primer—if all goes well. That sets the gun into double-action mode. By contrast, the M1911 is a single-action only gun. If the hammer on that model is down, cranking away at the trigger will accomplish precisely nothing beyond exercising your finger. When the hammer is cocked, the safety lever can be engaged, locking the action in place until it's released again.

Safety levers can be easy to work or a challenge, depending on where they're put and how they are to be operated. On a gun with a decocker, it's often best to lower the hammer and then turn off the safety, since the trigger weight is heavy enough to keep things from going off. On rifles such as the M1 Garand, the safety is a tab on the front end of the trigger guard that has to be pressed forward for the gun to fire.

Yet another example is a tang safety, the slider knob on the stock:

As always, there are variations to please the tinkerer's soul. If you give your character a particular kind of gun, you need to know the specific safeties or lack thereof that the model in question possesses. But the common guns carried by police officers, in the present or in many decades of the twentieth century, lack active safeties. In fact, a Colt or Smith & Wesson .38 Special revolver or a Glock make up the majority of handguns issued to cops. Unless your detective is carrying a Webley Fosbery, I don't want to hear about any safety levers being released on a wheelgun. The same is true about the Austrian Wonderpistol, the Glock. Often, in fact, guns that the police carry are double-action only, without the need for a safety. In New York City, law-enforcement Glocks have a New York trigger, made excessively heavy. This is the product of bureaucrats who fear machines that function easily, and given the lack of accuracy of NYPD officers, this is an example of focusing on the wrong thing.

The take-away message here is to know what you're giving your character. Look up the particular gun, and know how it works. Research is a part of the process, and your knowing readers will appreciate you for doing it.

Assault Rifles

So far, I've mostly stayed away from political matters, since the emphasis here is on what a writer needs to know to get gun facts correct in stories. But here, I'm wading into the thick and smelly. The subject is assault rifles.

First, let's dispose of another term that shows up in the media and elsewhere, the assault weapon. This is plainly silly. Any weapon can be used to attack. Any weapon can be used to defend. In fact, most weapons are good at both functions. That's especially true about most firearms. Some have advantages in one or the other area, and we'll get to those in a moment, but calling something an assault weapon is generally redundant. Certainly, this term has been exploited by advocates of gun control. Note in particular what Josh Sugarmann, currently the head of the Violence Policy Center, had to say in 1988 in a position paper:

> Assault weapons—just like armor-piercing bullets, machine guns, and plastic firearms—are a new topic. The weapons' menacing looks, coupled with the public's confusion over fully automatic machine guns versus semi-automatic assault weapons—anything that looks like a machine gun is assumed to be a machine gun—can only increase the chance of public support for restrictions on these weapons. In addition, few people can envision a practical use for these weapons.

But my job in these articles is to inform writers so as to remove confusion.

Moving on, then. Have a look at the classic military rifle at the start of the twentieth century:

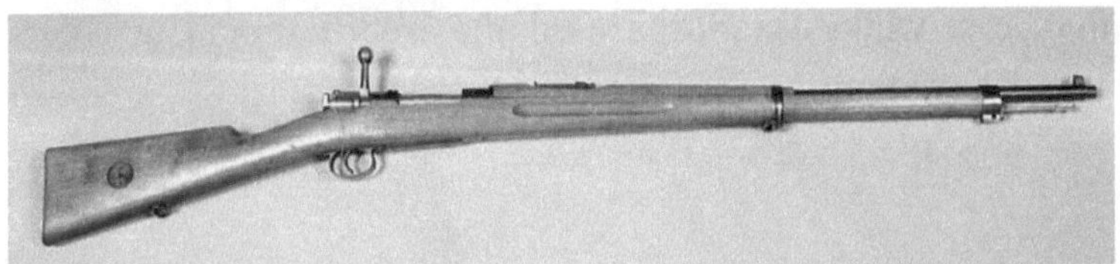

That's a Swedish Mauser that shoots a 6.5mm round. The rifle is fifty inches long. The Russian Mosin-Nagant was forty-eight inches. And that was typical for the standard infantry arm of the day. Yes, the Americans and the British were using rifles of around forty-four inches, but that's still lengthy.

There are advantages to this. As I mentioned before, a longer barrel gives the powder time to burn, thereby increasing the

velocity. A greater distance between the front and rear sights creates a longer sight radius. This doesn't affect the inherent accuracy of the gun, but it does make lining up a shot easier for the shooter—at least that's the idea. And military doctrine of the day expected soldiers to hit targets at considerable distance. Remember that generals always come prepared for the last war. The belief was that the common soldier should be able to fire aimed and effective shots at targets way over yonder. Consider, for example, the mad minute, a requirement of British soldiers to land shots in a four-foot circle at three-hundred yards in sixty seconds. The best score on record is thirty-six hits, done by Sergeant Major Jesse Wallingford in 1908. The story goes that during the Christmas peace in World War I, German officers remarked to their British counterparts that they were surprised about the Brits having so many machine guns, when actually the men were just firing the bolt-action SMLE.

But World War I bogged down into trenches, and the leaders needed a way to break out. Winston Churchill loved the idea of the tank, while Americans used the trench broom, a short-barreled shotgun, and the Germans toyed with this:

the Bergmann MP-18. It fired the 9mm Parabellum cartridge and thus was a submachine gun. We later developed our own in the form, the Thompson, known as the Tommy Gun.

The Russians tried this beast, the Fedorov avtomat from 1915:

It fired a full-power rifle cartridge, but its design was complicated.

A battle rifle cartridge is as powerful as it is for the purpose of penetrating armor and hitting targets at long ranges. But firing a lot of those rounds in a hurry isn't conducive to accuracy without a gun mount, and military thinkers were coming on the idea that when a lot of people are running at you quickly, you need to shovel the lead out. The distance involved won't be that much—under three hundred yards.

The need for this became apparent especially in World War II on the Eastern Front between Germany and the Soviet Union. The Germans had the Mauser K98, a shortened version of the Gewehr 98, their long battle rifle from the First World War, firing a full-power round, and the MP-40:

a submachine gun or machine pistol that shot the standard 9mm used in German handguns. But battle rifles are good for a thousand yards, and handguns do their

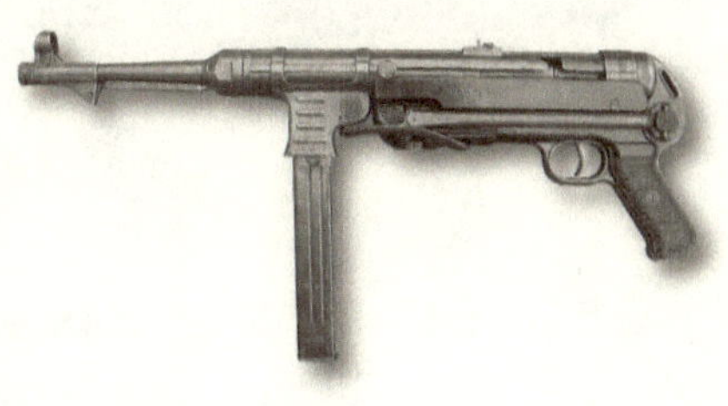

best work at talking distances. What about in between?

Introducing the MP-44:

It fired a bullet of 7.92mm from a case that was 33mm in length. The Mausers used 7.92 x 57 mm rounds. The notion there is that it's easier to retool if you're not changing the barrel diameter. But the reduced power of the cartridge allows for easier control of fully automatic fire necessary to stop mass attacks inside of three hundred yards. Hitler got a look at the gun and declared it a Sturmgewehr—literally an assault rifle. He loved adding "assault" to everything, but even though the thought about this weapon was defensive, being able to send a wall of bullets down range is useful in storming (the other translation of sturm) through an enemy's line, particularly in urban combat.

Are you thinking that the MP-44 looks familiar? How about this weapon:

If you think that the AK-47 looks a lot like the German rifle, you're not alone. In fact, lots of people other than Mikhail

Kalashnikov have said the same thing. The Russian gun shoots a 7.62 x 39 round, their battle rifle round being 7.62 x 54, has a detachable magazine with the distinctive curve required by the shape of the cartridge, and is made for the same purpose as the MP-44. The Russians declared, Oh my Marx, no, we didn't copy the German gun. Uh huh. It's length, by the way, is around thirty-five inches with the stock extended.

Americans, loving plastic and high-tech widgets, went for this ray gun:

the M-16, designed by Eugene Stoner, a man who had been working in the aircraft industry. It's made of plastic—excuse me, polymer—and aluminum and so forth, all with the purpose of reducing its weight. It shoots a 5.56 x 45 cartridge. In English units, that's a .22, a tiny round. General Curtis LeMay tried an early model out and figured it made a good primary weapon for air base security police, and some of our special forces units operating in Vietnam in the run up to our full involvement there liked it, so Robert McNamara and his bean counters—I mean whiz kids—decided to inflict the M-16 on everyone. Over time, the right combination of bullet weight and gunpowder were found to work with the design.

Today, the lines between submachine gun and assault rifle are getting blurred:

This dingus, a star of the later seasons of *Stargate SG-1*, shoots a pistol round that acts a lot like a lightweight rifle round that can't decide what it wants to be.

But what is an assault rifle? Remember that the goal of such a weapon is to facilitate rapid movement in close-quarters battle or to stop an enemy attempting such. That being the case, it has to have the following characteristics:

1. Intermediate cartridge

I've explained that here and there in this chapter, but the round is intermediate between the power of a handgun round and a battle rifle cartridge. It's not a .45 ACP, and it's not a .30-'06, but it wants to be able to do what both of those can do.

2. Detachable magazine

Changing out magazines is easier than pulling out stripper clips of rounds and shoving them into the fixed mag.

3. Selective fire

The weapon must be capable of semiautomatic fire—one trigger squeeze, one shot—and full-auto—keeps shooting till the trigger is released or the gun runs dry. Many of them also have a three-round burst setting. But without full-auto capability, it's not an assault rifle.

And that's the key point. In America, unless you have a Class III firearms license and all the paperwork and tax stamp, you can't legally own a full-auto gun. The AR-15, the semiautomatic only version of the M-16, is no different from any other semiautomatic rifle in its basic functioning, except that it looks funny. People who say otherwise are simply trying to cloud the issue. If your character is a chief of police who has to kowtow to the mayor, that person may refer to a gun as an assault rifle. If your character has an anti-gun agenda, the same is true. But you need to know the correct definitions so as to make sense when you're creating characterization.

Accuracy

Accuracy is an important concept in firearms, but it's one that's often misunderstood. For the vast majority of people who use guns, the weapon itself is more inherently or mechanically accurate than the user can take advantage of. This is true about any well-made firearm, be it a snub-nosed revolver or a rifle. This isn't to say that shooters are sloppy. It's just that the gun is capable of precision when locked down in a rest—a device that holds the gun for testing—that a human being can approach asymptotically while always having a little more improvement possible.

One thing that affects practical accuracy—the ability of the shooter to use the gun well—is the trigger. You don't even need a firearm to see how this is true. Hold out your dominant hand as if you're squeezing the grip of a handgun, and pretend to work the imaginary trigger. Notice how your hand moves. That's with a trigger that has no resistance whatsoever. The heavier the pull weight—the amount of force needed to get the thing all the way back to the point when the firing mechanism releases—the harder it will be to keep the sights aligned where you want them. Triggers that have to accomplish a lot inside the gun before that point are gritty or squishy or weighty. That can be overcome, but it will take work.

Barrels affect accuracy, and that's an element of the design that the user can't control any more than during the act of buying or assembling the gun. There are several ways to attach the barrel to the receiver—the part where the chamber at the barrel's rear end connects to the frame, and the chamber is where a cartridge is inserted and the bang happens. Barrels get hot when bullets are pushed down them by burning powder, so the user needs the equivalent of an oven mitt—called a handguard—to hold on to the forward part of the gun. But barrels vibrate like a wave, and if they're touching something, that distorts the aim. If it distorts the aim the same way every time, that's fine, but the trouble is that the distortion can seem random. Thus supremely accurate rifles have what is called a free-floating barrel with no points of contact past the receiver. This is not something that most fiction writers will spend much time with, but it's good to be aware of it just in case.

To return to what the user can do to muck up the aim, consider the sights. Most handguns have a squarish post at the muzzle end and some kind of a notched piece at the back—the front and rear sights. Focus on the front sight, align it in the middle of the notch at the rear, and squeeze without altering that alignment.

Another kind of sight, that used to be more common on rifles, are a ring at the rear and some kind of post at the front. These are called ghost-ring sights if the opening is fairly large and peep sights if the hole is tiny. It allows considerable accuracy, since the eye likes looking through an aperture, and it's just about as quick to align as the previous kind.

Then there are the scopes. That's a world unto itself, and if you're going to get into the details of how those work, you'll be exploring optics and physics and ophthalmology. For most purposes, it's enough to know that a scope magnifies—it's a telescope, after all—and there are lines inside that eliminate the need to focus on only the front sight and avoid the temptation to focus on the target or the rear sight. The trouble with a scope is that it draws the attention of the user, attention that might be better given to the charging lion coming from the side.

Now we've talked about bullets, but note here that longer, heavier, and pointier ones push through the wind more reliably than short, light, and blunt ones.

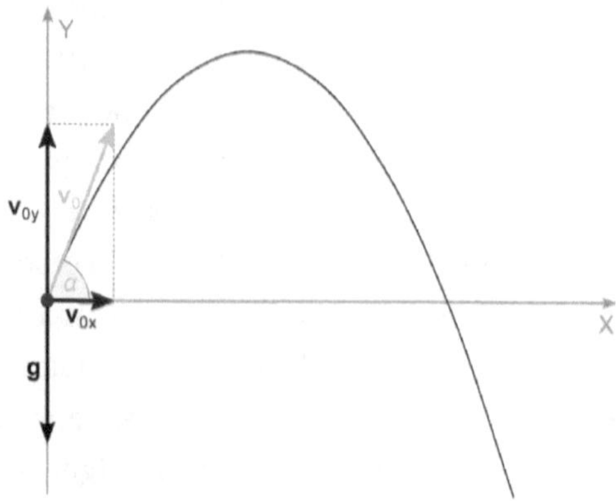

But the key point about bullets is that they do not travel in straight lines. Instead, thanks to the force of gravity and the resistance of air, they move in what is called a ballistic trajectory. That's a parabola, if you're mathematically inclined, or a rainbow if you need a cheerful image. The bullet emerges from the muzzle, rises a little, then arcs over and starts dropping. The longer it's in motion, the farther it will drop, if there's enough space between it and the ground.

Now why does it rise? The sights aren't in line with the barrel. On a handgun, for example, a straight line between the front and rear sight and a straight line through the barrel will intersect a little bit ahead of the muzzle and again at some fifty yards out. On rifles, those lines cross a second time farther out, and often, the sights are adjustable to change that intersection point.

If you imagine that rainbow moving left to right in front of you, the bullet starts near the top of the arc at the left when it comes out of the muzzle, rises above the line of the sights, goes across the top of the parabola, then drops back below the sight line. Higher velocities flatten out the left side of that arc and a bit into the right-hand side. Point blank range is a term that originally referred to the distance at which the white center of a traditional bull's eye—white in French is *blanc*—can be struck without altering the sights. For a handgun, that distance is again some fifty yards. Rifles generally have a point-blank range of a hundred to three hundred yards.

All of this is to say that you can be as accurate as you like about accuracy. How much you need for your story is for you to decide. These are the basics and should be enough to be getting on with for most characters and plots.

The Safety Rules

I discussed mechanical safeties in a previous chapter. Now, I offer my take on the Four Rules of Gun Safety, as taught to us by the late Jeff Cooper, Marine Lt. Colonel, firearms instructor, and essayist:

1. Treat all guns as loaded.

Now we sometimes have to look down the barrel to check the rifling or the results of cleaning, and we have to know for dang sure that we unloaded the thing, but as long as the piece is a gun—in other words, as long as the action is closed and the dingus is assembled—I'm going to check it by looking in the chamber—from the rear end, not looking down the muzzle—and in the magazine or cylinder for ammunition.

2. Never let the muzzle cover anything that you're not willing to destroy.

Remember how all guns are treated as loaded? Don't point guns at people in jest. Don't aim at the cat and pretend to fire. Don't sweep the gun across a room full of people at a gun show, and don't aim at your neighbor's wall. There are times when this rule is difficult to apply fully, since we have to point the muzzle somewhere, but always choose the least bad option if no good one is available.

3. Keep your finger off the trigger and out of the trigger guard until your sights are on the target.

Even Hollywood is getting this one right lately. Look at characters who keep their index fingers straight along the gun's frame while moving around. The point here is that barring mechanical failure or something else getting hung up in the trigger guard, that gun cannot fire unless the trigger is squeezed. If your finger doesn't touch the trigger, nothing will happen.

4. Identify your target, what's around it, and what's behind it.

Sometimes, we miss. Sometimes, a bullet goes through the target and on to what's on the other side, particularly the full-metal jacket or the high-speed varieties. Don't shoot at a shadow or a sound.

Various organizations have ten commandments, and any gun safety manual will offer you pages of text, much of it in red,

on this subject, but really, those four rules cover just about any possible situation in which a person with a firearm could muck things up. Follow those four, and you're highly unlikely ever to discharge a firearm unintentionally or to cause excessive harm by doing so.

But since these articles are aimed at writers, now let's discuss the implications of these rules for your characters. When a novice picks up a gun, the person often immediately waves the thing around, finger on the trigger, and sometimes squeezes without thinking. A trained person, by contrast, takes care with this object of power. Many readers won't notice anything of significance in how you describe your character manipulating a firearm, but those in the know will pick up on it, and if the description of handling doesn't match the way you've portrayed your character in other regards, that will make us irritated. It's not good to irritate readers in the know.

Of course, also remember that these Four Rules were formulated in the seventies and arose out of Cooper's teaching in the couple of decades before that. A character in a western will operate under a different standard. Many of them will be drunk or grouchy, and the consequences of killing someone without meaning it weren't always the same as today. If you're writing about someone in the Second World War, find a copy of the firearms training manual or similar to learn the rules as they were given then. A rebellious character may ignore even those, naturally.

The point here is that how your character handles a firearm tells your readers about that person and about you as a researcher.

Guns: The Hollywood Edition

Every once in a while, it's a good idea to look at how things are done wrong. With that in mind, I present to you Hollywood guns, in which we find out that Tinseltown is peeing on our shoes and calling it a submarine movie.

1. Racking the action

In this picture, we see the slide on a semiautomatic pistol pulled back to allow a round to be loaded into the chamber. That's as should be. That's what has to be done. Once that's done, the gun is ready to go. But Hollywood

can't avoid having characters perform that action repeatedly. Every time they want to threaten someone, they whip out pistols and point about the room until the intended victim mouths off, at which time every gun from a snub-nosed revolver to a howitzer produces a clack-clack sound.

What that means is that unless a shell is ejected, the gun didn't have a round chambered beforehand, and the victim could have waltzed over and taken the weapon. Yes, the Israelis teach their commandos to carry without a round loaded, but I suspect that's because they had to take whatever kind of gun they could get their hands on in early days, so rules about safeties on some guns but not others would have been confusing. But most people carry their guns ready to go.

2. Suppressors

These are often called silencers, but that's wrong. They only reduce the volume by a few tens of decibels—enough to save the shooter from hearing damage, but not enough to make the firearm whisper. And if the ammunition is supersonic, the bullet going down range will create a sonic boom.

But in film, every gun can be made to sound like a cat sneezing with a quarter-inch tube on the end of the barrel. That includes revolvers, even though most such guns have a gap between the cylinder and the barrel, allowing the cylinder to turn. Gases escape from that gap—a significant source of noise that can't be suppressed. Suppressors also change the point of impact and the velocity of the bullet, which means that the sights have to be set for suppressed firing.

The truth is that some guns can be made very quiet, but the size of the suppressor needed makes carrying the thing inconvenient. And if it's a self-loading firearm, the operation of the machine itself makes a lot of noise.

3. Sound

When not suppressed, guns are loud. We're talking a rock concert with the speakers turned up to eleven. Actually, they're louder than that. And for some reason, Hollywood thinks that setting off firearms inside concrete buildings isn't bad for one's hearing.

Huh?

4. Magazine size

Gun control freaks go on and on about how many rounds should be allowed in a magazine. It's fifteen here, ten there, and seven was tried in New York. That's until they decide to demand only one at a time. I

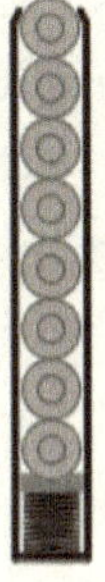

suspect that's because they see movies in which bad guys have firearms with infinite capacities. Sometimes, the good guys do as well. And they keep shooting on full-auto for minutes at a time without having to reload—or without the barrels melting.

But that's plain wrong. Typical pistol magazines run from seven rounds in older M1911s to fifteen or seventeen in many Berettas and Glocks. Revolvers have five or six. Even the banana magazine of the AK-47 holds only thirty. The rate of fire of a full-auto gun varies with the model, but they're in the hundreds to more than a thousand rounds a minute. A semiautomatic firearm launches only one round per squeeze of the trigger, so it's up to the user how long that takes. A magazine can be emptied in seconds, if emptying your gun is the only goal. Now there are things like this:

But those have a habit of jamming. And they're hard to carry, especially if you have to conceal them.

5. Aim

Guns have to be aimed. Yes, if you plan to spray and pray, you can hold your grease gun at your hip and let go, but to score one-shot hits on a desired target, you have to use the sights. Or practice every day with lots of rounds and get really close. Just blasting away is a fine method for wasting ammunition and hitting bystanders, a technique practiced by the NYPD. This is especially true if you hold your handgun sideways, gangsta style.

6. Knockdown power

Newton informed us that for every action, there is an equal and opposite reaction. That means that if your bullet knocks down the guy you're shooting at, you get knocked down when you fire the gun. Now it is true that some people get hit while they're running and off-balance and thus fall over when shot, and others drop to the ground out of surprise, but the bullet itself cannot shove someone over.

Along the same lines, and as discussed elsewhere, the more powerful the round, the more punishing it is to shoot, especially in lightweight guns. And unless the shooter has exceptional luck, one shot from a pipsqueak handgun isn't going to stop an assailant.

7. Sturm und Drang

When a bullet hits something, what happens to the target? It explodes, naturally. Well, actually, no, it doesn't. Unless it's made of nitroglycerin. Even if the target is drenched in gasoline, it's not likely to flare up. So no, you can't make a car go up in a ball of fire by shooting its tank.

8. Carry

Remember Agent Smith in The Matrix? Or Ivan Chekhov in Boondock Saints? They were big guys. But even so, those Desert Eagles they carried are huge guns. We're talking about a foot long and more than four pounds in weight. You ain't hiding one of those in your sock. It's not even going to be concealed under a tailored suit coat. You're going to need a big cape or a tent-sized shirt to hide one of those. As discussed elsewhere, carrying a gun in a sensible manner takes work, but understand that if it looks huge when you draw it, it's going to feel huge when you're carrying it.

9. Anachronisms

John Wayne is the quintessential western character. But in just about every western he starred in, he carried an 1873 Colt Single Action Army revolver and a 1892 Winchester rifle. But *The Searchers*, for example, starts in 1868. That's a neat trick. But it's not unique to westerns. In *Titanic*, David Warner's character packs an M1911, though at that time, such pistols were just getting going as a military firearm. It would have been more accurate to give him a Colt Pocket Hammerless, but that's a small gun and doesn't look as impressive.

What's the point here? Surprise, surprise, surprise, Hollywood engages in trickery when it comes to guns. And that's part of why I've written this book. You, dear writers, need to know what the truth is about firearms: what's possible, what's reasonable in how they're used, and what's just blowing smoke.

Glocks

The previous chapter left out a brand of gun that is abused by writers so often that it deserves attention all by itself. I'm talking about the Austrian Combat Tupperware, otherwise known as the Glock.

The manufacturer, founded by Gaston Glock, originally sold knives and shovels (called entrenching tools) to the Austrian military, a fighting force noted for, well, um, defending the neutrality of Austria. Said organization's most famous member was Captain von Trapp, who commanded a submarine and went on to wear an eye patch and deliver lines of Shakespeare in Klingon—no, wait, that was Christopher Plummer and von Trapp's naval days were in the time before Austria went on a diet as a nation and became a landlocked country.

The Austrians were using this, the Walther P38, a double action/single action handgun developed shortly before the Second World War. The Walther also provided the basis for the Beretta 92, a handgun that replaced the excellent M1911 in much of the U.S. military. The Austrians wanted a new pistol that would be drop-safe (for purposes of surrendering without getting hurt?), that would be easy to maintain, and that would hold a bunch of 9mm Luger cartridges.

Glock hadn't made a firearm before 1982, but he was an engineer with sixteen designs to his name, so why not take a shot at the contract? This is what he came up with:

It uses the tilting-barrel, locked-breech action that John Moses Browning used in his last pistol design, the Browning Hi Power. The frame is made of polymer (read plastic), while the slide is steel, treated originally in a process called Tenifer—though not anymore. The original magazine capacity was seventeen rounds, but that had no relation to the fact that the pistol is called the Glock 17. There are Glock numbers into the forties now, and those numbers have no obvious pattern with regard to how many rounds are on board or what caliber they are.

What was new? Not much, actually. The Heckler & Koch VP70 was the first polymer handgun, released in 1970. But that

didn't win the attention of many, possibly due to its odd looks and clunky trigger.

Glocks use a striker mechanism instead of a hammer, but that's also not original, at least in firearms generally. In fact, it goes back to the Dreyse needle gun designed in the early part of the nineteenth century. Bolt-action rifles use the same mechanism, a spring-loaded pin that strikes the primer when released, and a number of handguns also used strikers for many decades before Glock came along.

In other words, Glock pulled together a number of good ideas into one gun. Another requirement of the Austrian military was a pistol that would stand up to lots of use and abuse, and despite reports of catastrophic failures when poor quality ammunition is used, the gun does have a reputation for surviving torture, and Glocks have earned the love of YouTube celebrity, Hickok45. Here in America, we can get Glocks in 9mm Luger, .357 Sig, .40 S&W, 10mm, .45 GAP, and .45 ACP. There is a Glock 18, a full-auto version of the Model 17, but good luck owning one of those, and there are three models in .380 ACP, but thanks to the Gun Control Act of 1968, two of the three lowest-power models aren't allowed for sale to ordinary citizens. The "reasons" for that are arcane.

The preceding is what a Glock is. But what is it not? Let me quote Officer John McClane in *Die Hard 2*:

"That punk pulled a Glock 7 on me. You know what that is? It's a porcelain gun made in Germany. Doesn't show up on your airport X-ray machines, here, and it costs more than you make in a month."

What did he get right? The part about some guy being a punk. The rest of it is flat wrong.

1. Glock 7

There is no Glock 7. Well, the best I can figure is that Glock's seventh patent was for a piezoelectric device for circuit boards. Quite the punk to pull out one of those.

2. Porcelain gun

Um, no. There are guns being printed out of plastic these days, but those only work for a few rounds before blowing up. A porcelain gun would be better known as a grenade.

3. Made in Germany

Glocks are made in Austria and in the United States, with a few made in Uruguay and Taiwan.

4. X-ray machines

Glocks do show up on airport X-ray machines and are detected by metal detectors. The polymer is opaque to X-rays, and the steel slide and barrel will make the TSA molester's wand beep.

5. Cost

I don't know what Chief Lorenzo's salary was, but Glocks go for between $500 and $600 typically, depending on options and where you buy them.

The common error that McClane failed to include was the notion of a Glock safety. Recall the lever dingus on the trigger that we discussed earlier? That's the only external safety on the pistol. There are also a firing pin safety and a drop safety inside, but no one flicks those off except by squeezing the trigger. If anyone refers to a safety that must be turned off before the gun can be fired, said writer had better call it the Cominolli safety lever or a Siderlock button, aftermarket modifications that are available. But those are not common, and most Glock users either understand how to keep their fingers off the trigger and out of the trigger guard when holstering the weapon, or they add an extra orifice in their feet. The police in the City of New York (NYPD) require a twelve-pound trigger to be installed as another form of safety, instead of the standard 5.5 lbs. trigger, but we see how they do on marksmanship. The standard trigger has two stages, but it's a lot shorter than a double-action pull. The pistols are wide and feel like something you'd pick up at a hardware store, but they are lightweight, and the subcompact and compact models do snuggle into an inside-the-waistband holster without too much difficulty.

What's the point here? Glocks, just like all other firearms, are designs with a set of characteristics that a writer must understand before including them in stories. Reporters in particular would benefit from such knowledge, but they are distinctly resistant to learning about guns.

Colt Single Action Army

This is one of the definitive firearms of the Old West, the Colt Single Action Army revolver, first on the market in 1873. John Wayne carried a version with him in many of his movies, and General Patton had his with ivory grips when he wanted to be on display. (But Patton only ever carried one SAA. His other revolver was a Smith & Wesson .357 Registered Magnum.)

The mystique suits the gun. It was a single-action revolver, weighing 2.3 pounds, more or less, depending on the barrel length, and came originally in a 7.5 inch barrel. The artillery model was better at 5.5 inches, since it cleared leather quicker. But the absurd model (lower left), supposedly a Buntline Special, didn't exist until long after the days of the Old West were long gone.

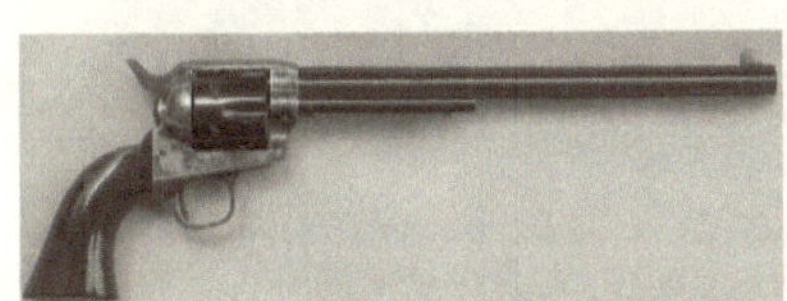

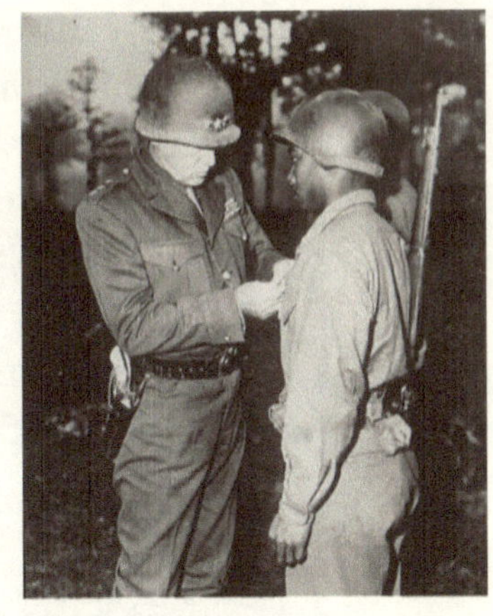

They had six chambers in the cylinder, loaded by putting the hammer on half-cock, opening the loading gate on the right-hand side, inserting one round, skipping a chamber, then inserting four more rounds, and finishing by closing the loading gate and pulling back the hammer to full cock, then dropping it onto the empty chamber at the top. This was because the SAA had the firing pin on the hammer with no means of keeping it off the live cartridge. Legend has it that pistoleroes stuffed funeral money into the empty chamber.

The Army used it with the .45 Colt round, a 250 grain bullet atop 40 grains of black powder for a typical velocity of 900 feet per second, plus or minus again depending on barrel length. Another popular caliber was the .44-40 Winchester that could be used in the Winchester 1873 lever-action rifle. This simplified logistics in the wilderness if a person only had to carry one type of ammunition for two guns. Later came .32-20, .22 Long Rifle, and

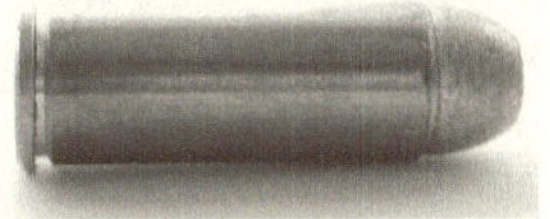

eventually just about every revolver caliber.They were carried in holsters from the Civil War that covered the gun with a flap, but those slowed down the draw, and people carrying these brutes learned to bend the flap backward and cut a hole in it to form an

open-top model:and that is the image that most often comes to mind.

And lest you think that this is a gun of the Old West only, Ruger makes several Blackhawk models. Several Italian companies make reproductions as well, and Colt is making the Single Action Army again. When something works this well, it's bound to last.

Colt Navy

The last chapter gave images of the Colt Single Action Army. But while that revolver is the one that comes to mind for a lot of people when they think of the Old West and handguns, there's an earlier Colt that was the handy pistol to have around in 1851 and many decades after that: the Colt Navy.

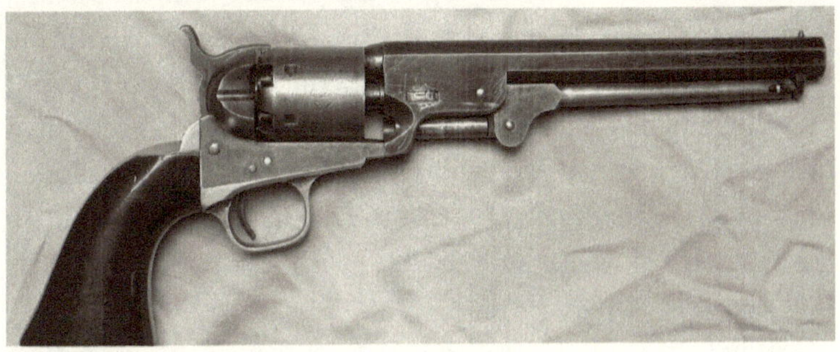

Unlike the SAA, this one was designed by Samuel Colt himself. Colt's first pistol, the Paterson, had been overly complicated and fragile, and his first company went out of business. His next models, the Walker and the Dragoon, were massive pieces better suited for saddle guns. He also came out with pocket revolvers starting in 1847, but those were small-caliber backup pieces.

By contrast, the Navy—so-called because a scene from the Battle of Campeche, a victory of ships from Texas and the Yucatan against the Mexican navy—weighed in at 2.6 pounds and measuring thirteen inches in length. It shot a .36 caliber ball at something like a thousand feet per second and a 140 grain conical bullet at a somewhat slower speed, putting it in the same class as today's .380 or .38 Special, the latter being the gun that was the sidearm of police officers for a long time.

It was a cap and ball revolver with an octagonal barrel. The rear sight was a notch cut into the forward part of the hammer that could be used only when the hammer was cocked. But owners found that the Navy pointed well, feeling like an extension of the arm. Loading it required pulling the hammer to half-cock, then pouring powder down the front of the chambers, ramming a bullet home on top of the powder with the loading lever beneath the barrel, and putting a percussion cap on the cones at the rear of the cylinder. After the Civil War, the arrival of self-contained metallic cartridges made the older system obsolete, and many bought conversion cylinders for their pistols. Clint Eastwood demonstrates this in *The Good, the Bad, and the Ugly*, though since the movie takes place during the Civil War, that's an anachronism.

Many of the Confederate generals, as well as lots of soldiers of all ranks, including especially the cavalry, carried Navys as their sidearm. Captain Quantrill and his raiders liked their

handiness and multiple shots before reloading. The practice was to carry two on their belts and two in saddle holsters. That latter habit is shown in the "Fill your hand, you son of a bitch!" scene in *True Grit*, Rooster Cogburn having been a member (albeit fictional) of Quantrill's company.

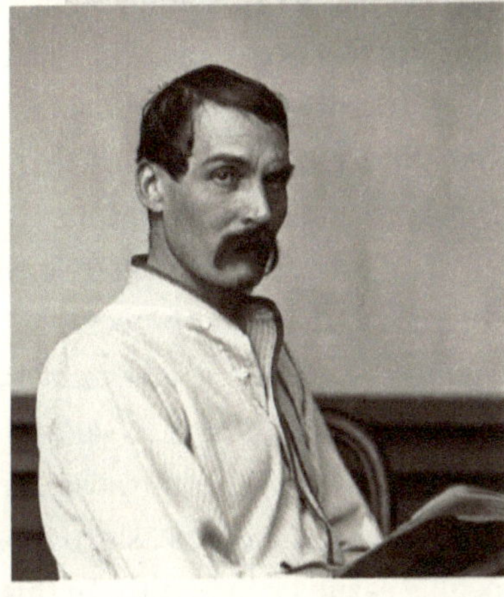

Ned Kelly (left), the Australian outlaw, and Richard Francis Burton right), English author and adventurer, both carried them. But the iconic owner of Colt Navys was James Butler Hickok, better known as Wild Bill:

He wore them in cavalry style with the butts forward—note the ivory grips here. From what I've read, it appears that he didn't use a cross-draw technique, but would twist his hands inward to grip the pistols and then twist back out and pull upward. My own practice of this method leads me to believe that it facilitated cocking the hammers rapidly. Alas, he probably used a Colt Army revolver in his duel with Dave Tutt in Springfield, Missouri, but the Navys are what are identified with him.

Two more points before we leave this. My western character, Henry Dowland (actually, I suspect his name is John Henry Dowland, but he won't admit to that) carries two of his own that he's named Alpha and Omega.

A friend of mine told me that he'd read about someone in the Old West naming his guns that way, and I liked the idea, since Dowland quotes from Scripture as any good devil is able to do.

The other thing to note is that the Navy figures into one of the racist efforts at gun control in the Reconstruction era south. Tennessee passed a law in 1879, referred to as the Army and Navy Law, banning the sale of any pistol other than the Colt Army or Navy. The purpose for this was to keep freed blacks from buying handguns, since those two each cost more than poor people earned in a month. In this regard, nothing much changes.

The Colt Navy is a beautiful pistol from an era when elegance counted for a lot, but it was also a working tool. And the good news is that they are being made even today by several companies—but not Colt.

Sharps

The popular image of guns of the Old West has it that everyone went about with a Winchester 1873 lever-action rifle and a Colt Single Action Army as a sidearm. But the reality is more complicated. A whole lot of the activity happened before 1873, and there were many other guns doing work west of the Mississippi.

One of them was the Sharps rifle:

It was designed by a fellow named Christian Sharps—you're surprised, right? The patent came in 1848, and the rifle in 1851. That's the same year that the Colt Navy was sold for the first time, making that a good year.

From the first, it was a large-bore precision rifle, aimed at hitting targets at long range, whether we're talking enemy soldiers or large animals. The Sharps was a single-shot, originally in .44 caliber, though .52 became the standard. It was used as a sniper rifle with a Malcolm scope by the sharpshooters under Hiram Berdan's command, though the rifles were used on both sides, especially in the shorter carbine version favored by cavalry troopers, including my western character, Henry Dowland.

Unlike most infantry rifles, the Sharps was a breech-loader. The trigger guard acted as a lever that dropped the breech block, opening the rear of the barrel.

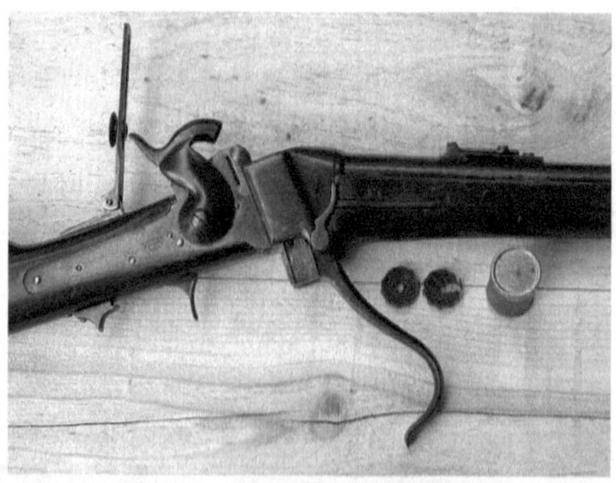

A paper or linen cartridge was then inserted. A Maynard tape primer was installed on many of these, working something like a modern cap gun. Closing the action cut the rear end of the cartridge to expose the powder inside. These rifles were often

converted after the Civil War to .50-70 or .50-90 metallic cartridges—that means .50 caliber and seventy or ninety grains of black powder shoving along a bullet of some 400 or 500 grains at around 1,400 feet per second, an ounce of lead chugging along at a good rate.

As such, they were the classic buffalo gun. The accuracy potential of the rifle was enhanced with tang sights and a set trigger on some models. Squeezing the rear trigger set the front trigger to a lightweight pull, necessitating less effort and thus less disturbance of the aim in firing.

These features show up in various films, notably *Quigley Down Under* and the 2010 version of *True Grit*. Billy Dixon, a scout for the U. S. Army, used one in real life to shoot an Indian who was part of the siege at the Adobe Walls outpost in northern Texas. The range was 1,578 yards. Dixon said it was a lucky shot, but the besiegers figured that they didn't have a chance and gave up.

Until the advent of smokeless powder, the Sharps was one of the most powerful firearms going. And the good news is that companies are making reproductions today.

Laws of the Internet

Those of us who spend much time arguing the question of gun rights on the Internet often run into examples of Markley's Law in action. What is Markley's Law, my non-gun-enthusiast readers may be asking?

> Markley's Law: The adage that any Internet discussion regarding firearm owners will eventually mention male genitalia.

Generally, this takes the form of someone who supports gun control claiming that gun owners are compensating for small anatomy. But obsession with penises isn't the only defect of personality to be found in those who yearn to violate the rights of others. Submitted for your consideration is a new law, based on many observations:

> As t (time) increases, the probability that a gun control supporter will make a sexist or homophobic remark about a gun rights advocate during a discussion on guns approaches 1.

This observation is all the more interesting since gun control supporters tend to be on the left of the American political spectrum, and thus such language would be unacceptable by their fellows in any other context.

Epilogue

As you've seen, the Gun Nut Forest is a vast territory. One book can't cover everything. What I hope this one has done for you is provide an entry for writers who want realism in their stories. I've mentioned sources throughout that are opportunities to learn more. Time for some shameless commerce, as the Car Talk guys called it.

My co-author, Ranjit Singh, and I have a book that focuses on the political aspects of guns in America. Journalists are the primary audience, but their job depends on the ability to tell compelling stories. If you're concerned with politics and guns in your fiction, *Each One, Teach One* gives more discussion of the topic.

In any case, thank you for the time you have given to this book. Now get back to writing.

Greg Camp was born in the hills of North Carolina about a hundred thirty years later than was good for him. He has wandered around the southern United States ever since, picking up bits of experience and polishing his curmudgeonly persona. He listens to the Muses whenever they sing to him. Following a star brought him and his cats to northwest Arkansas, where he has found safe harbor.

gregcampnc@gmail.com

@gregcampnc

https://medium.com/

www.patreon.com/gregcampnc

www.ingramcontent.com/pod-product-compliance
Lightning Source LLC
Chambersburg PA
CBHW031407250726

48656CB00002B/574